THE
50 PMP® EXAM
PREP QUESTIONS
EVERYONE GETS ~~RIGHT~~ WRONG

MASTER THE HARD QUESTIONS - ACE YOUR PMP EXAM

CORNELIUS FICHTNER, PMP

PM✦Exam Simulator™   PM✦PrepCast™

Get in touch:
OSP International LLC
8502 E Chapman Ave, Suite 349
Orange, CA 92869 USA
Email: support@pm-prepcast.com
Internet: www.osp-international.com

A book by Cornelius Fichtner
Published by: OSP International LLC

ISBN: 978-0-9964060-7-9

Thank you to everyone on the OSP International LLC team who helped bring this book to life. Special thanks to Stas Podoxin, Jeff Furman, and Elizabeth Harrin for being central and instrumental in ensuring that we have the most challenging questions and the best explanations.

Writing a book is one thing, but knowing that you have written a book that will genuinely help people is the pinnacle. Thank you, Oliver Lehmann, for endorsing the book.

To my beautiful wife, Shawn Pendley. Thank you for your unwavering love and support over the past 30 years (and for ignoring the post-it notes on every wall of our home).

CONTENTS

WELCOME!

You're here because you are preparing for your Project Management Professional (PMP)® exam, and you know the value of preparation.

You already know that sample exam questions are the key to confident preparation. Students tell us time and time again that practicing with an exam simulator and reviewing the answers is a practical technique for building confidence and knowledge.

Think of this book as your guide to making the most of the sample exam questions you have access to. You'll learn the three-step approach for studying with sample tests:

1. Prepare
2. Test
3. Check

The first section of this book covers the Prepare step. You'll learn how to avoid some of the pitfalls that students before you have fallen into. You'll revise the most challenging topics from our experience and training materials so you'll be prepared to face even the tough questions on your exam day. You'll also learn test taking strategies to help you recognize and answer any type of question.

The next section of this book covers the Test step. Here, you have the 50 toughest questions taken from The PM Exam Simulator (https://www.pm-exam-simulator.com), our flagship product that has helped thousands of students practice in realistic exam conditions.

Read and answer the questions, using the downloadable worksheet provided for your responses at **https://www.pm-exam-simulator.com/50answers**.

The third step is where you will complete the Check step and review your answers. This section of the book contains detailed explanations for each of the 50 questions. You'll be able to review whether you got the answer right and – more importantly – why the correct answer was the right choice.

This section contains references to the materials that will help you understand the topic at a deeper level. This step is so important for building the thorough knowledge of project management concepts that you'll need to confidently face any question on your exam.

Once you've worked through these 50 questions, you may feel like you'd benefit from more exam practice.

PM Exam Simulator™

HERE IS YOUR PM EXAM SIMULATOR DISCOUNT

As a thank you for purchasing this book, we have a special offer just for you:

You can get access to our premium PM Exam Simulator containing 2,100+ questions in five exams, with complete references and explanations, at a discounted price.

Simply navigate to
https://www.pm-exam-simulator.com/50coupon
to learn how to claim your discount.

PART ONE

Prepare Yourself

You've picked up this book because you want to prepare thoroughly for the PMP exam, and you know the value of reviewing sample questions as a practical way to build your knowledge and confidence.

In this section, you'll find:

- Explanations of the different types of questions you'll meet on the exam
- The top ten topic areas that students struggle with on sample exams, drawn from the data from thousands of students taking our mock tests and studying with our materials for their exam.

To make the most of your exam prep time, read through the different types of questions and familiarize yourself with each.

Then, read through the tough topic areas and see which of them feel challenging to you. Make a note to fully review these topics as part of your study plan.

PMP Exam Question Types

Your PMP exam will include a variety of different question types and to prepare thoroughly you should familiarize yourself with them all.

The question types are:

- Situational
- Knowledge-based
- Interpretational
- Technique-based
- Formula

I've read hundreds of forum posts from successful students and received hundreds of messages sharing exam stories, and I can tell you that the vast majority of questions you'll see on the exam are situational questions. You are guaranteed to get a wide selection of this type of assessment on your test.

So what is a situational question?

Let's look at what they are and how you can tackle them effectively.

Situational Questions

Situational questions may present you with scenarios containing both relevant and irrelevant information, which means they take longer to read and understand. And when time is at a premium in the exam room, that can be stressful.

The idea behind this is that in real life, you are often provided both relevant and irrelevant information. Your task is to identify what is important, ignore what does not matter and then act upon the real issues.

A single word can be critical, such as NOT or EXCEPT or ONLY or ALWAYS, which can change the meaning of the question or a choice.

Often, situational questions will have two answer choices that may appear to be reasonably correct. Therefore, it is vital that you identify what the question is asking. Based on the question and your knowledge of project management concepts, you must find the BEST answer.

Try not to fixate on the fact that 'this would never happen in the real world'. Remember that the situational question aims to test how you apply the theoretical knowledge. Focus on answering the question with the given information and your project management knowledge.

Let's review seven tips for preparing to answer situational questions.

1. Read the question
2. Identify the most important information
3. Read the answer choices in reverse order
4. Look for critical words
5. Work out what *PMBOK® Guide* terms are missing
6. Eliminate the obviously wrong answers
7. Don't overthink it

1. Read the question

It might sound simple, but under the pressure of the clock, many students fail to get answers right simply because they skimmed through the question and didn't truly understand what was being asked.

2. Identify the most important information

Next, pick out the most important data points and information in the question. There's often no 'perfect' answer to any situation, so look at what data you have and make a judgment call based on your project management knowledge.

3. Read the answer choices in reverse order

Read the answer choices twice: once down the list and next, in reverse order. Mixing up how you read the choices forces your brain to think differently and you might spot things you missed the first-time round.

4. Look for critical words

The PMP exam does not use formatting for critical words. For example, you will never see a word in capital letters, bold or italics on the exam.

Look at the structure of the question and identify words like 'not', 'except', 'only' and 'always' as those can change the meaning of a question or answer choice.

5. Work out what *PMBOK® Guide* terms are missing

If you've studied the *PMBOK® Guide* and are familiar with the terminology, it might surprise you to know that many problems on the exam don't include the vocabulary that is now ingrained in your brain.

When you are reading the question, think about what it is describing and whether you might have learned about it under a different name. Often, people at work will not use PMI terminology because they aren't familiar with it, so the exam reflects that.

If you are struggling to understand what's being asked, think about if it could be described in a different way and you might land on a term that helps you answer the question.

6. Eliminate the obviously wrong answers

There are normally a couple of answers that stand out as being obviously wrong, or definitely not the best course of action. It's impossible to provide 'rules' that will always work, but to give you an example, if an answer talks about ignoring the issue or escalating it to another manager, those could be choices to avoid.

Project managers are expected to be able to act in a leadership capacity, so it's nearly always better to see if there is an answer choice that relies on the PM taking some kind of action.

7. Don't overthink it

Try not to overthink the situation. A real-life situation may have a multitude of factors and considerations that cannot be represented in a single exam question. Try not to think of too many 'what if', 'what about' scenarios.

Focus on answering the question within the scope of the information provided and your project management knowledge. Don't spend too much time worrying about alternatives; just go with what is in the question.

You may see other types of questions on the exam as well, and it's worth knowing about those so you can prepare yourself, although experience tells us that you probably won't face that many alternative question types.

Regardless, it's important to prepare in a rounded way so you're ready for whatever you see on the test paper.

Knowledge-Based Questions

Knowledge-based questions are usually based on the *PMBOK® Guide* or project management concepts.

Students both love and hate knowledge-based questions. Some students like these questions because if you study the *PMBOK® Guide* well, you should be able to handle the majority of these questions easily. Students who lack preparation (and you obviously do not fall into this category, since you are reading this book) do not like this type of question, because they can easily be confused by unfamiliar terminology.

You also have to watch out for the minority of questions that are not directly covered in the *PMBOK® Guide*.

Interpretational Questions

Interpretational questions test your ability to deduce a situation or condition from the description of a status or problem. For example, you may be shown a graph or performance metric, and then you have to be able to determine if a good, bad or neutral/indifferent interpretation applies.

Some earned value management questions fall into this category, for example, interpreting the project performance based on the results of a calculation.

To prepare for interpretational questions, you must be actively thinking while studying the *PMBOK® Guide*. Ask yourself, "What would a positive vs. negative outcome look like?"

Technique-Based Questions

According to the *PMBOK® Guide*, a technique is "a defined systematic procedure employed by a human resource to perform an activity to produce a product or result or deliver a service, and that may employ one or more tools."

Almost every project management concept in the *PMBOK® Guide* has a corresponding technique, and it's likely that you'll encounter questions that test your understanding of them.

It may be knowledge-based where you can demonstrate your understanding of what a technique is used for, but you may also come across questions that test your understanding of how a technique is applied.

For example, you should know how to read and interpret a network diagram. You may be asked to do a forward pass or backward pass to demonstrate your understanding of the critical path method.

Our best advice is to review the tools and techniques covered by the *PMBOK® Guide* and to understand each one, its purpose, and how it is used. Some tools and techniques are easier to grasp. For example, brainstorming is familiar and intuitive and most students probably have used this technique on their projects. However, understanding how to do a forward or backward pass through a network diagram will require more study and attention.

Formula-Based Questions

Recent lessons learned feedback from those who have taken the exam indicates that there are almost no formula questions on the exam. However, PMI updates the balance of questions all the time, so we can't predict exactly what you will see on your test.

The most likely type of a formula question you'll get is where you may have to perform a simple calculation and then interpret the result. It's unlikely that you will need a calculator. Instead, you will have to make a judgement about what the result is telling you and what the most appropriate next steps would be, given that result. Alternatively, you may be given an earned value metric and will be required to interpret its meaning without the need to apply any formula or perform any calculation. For example, "The CPI on your project is 0.91. What is your best course of action?"

Formula-based questions are not just about finding an average, solving for the median or calculating earned value.

Understanding each element of the formula provides you with critical decision-making criteria to know which figures or information mentioned in the question should be included in the calculation. A good grasp of the formulas will speed up your time to answer the questions, as you can quickly eliminate any answer choices that are clear incorrect.

There are some tips for answering formula-based questions in Part 4.

Ten Topics Everyone Gets Wrong on the PMP Exam

We've supported thousands of students to succeed at the PMP exam, and as the company behind one of the most popular and trusted exam simulators on the market, we have a lot of data to share about the trickiest topics on the test.

In this section, we'll dive into the ten topics everyone gets wrong on their PMP exam.

OK, not absolutely everyone, but lots of people!

And after you've read this, you won't get them wrong, because you're going to learn what to look out for and how to respond to even the hardest questions on your assessment.

We've dug into the data and pulled out the results from thousands of mock PMP exams. We've spoken to our experienced trainers who have spent hundreds of hours delivering classroom courses. Here's a list of the ten toughest topics:

1. Which data analysis technique to use when
2. How to handle change requests
3. The best tools to measure project progress
4. The stages of team performance
5. The difference between parametric and analogous estimating
6. How to calculate expected monetary value
7. How to start a project
8. What goes into a work breakdown structure (WBS)
9. How to manage risk in agile sprints
10. How to close a project

The next section of this book will give you practical tips for answering all kinds of exam questions, including situational questions.

Let's review each of those tough topics.

1. Which data analysis technique to use when

The question that is answered incorrectly most often in the PM Exam Simulator is about data analysis techniques. In fact, data analysis features a couple of times in our review of the hardest questions.

Why people get it wrong

There are lots of different data analysis techniques and at first glance they can seem like they do very similar things. You have to know what each one is and how to apply it. More than that, it's important to be able to recognize what the situational question is talking about and what technique would be the best fit for the scenario.

What you can do to get it right

Study the different types of data analysis and how they are used. Here's a summary of the types of data analysis techniques you could find mentioned on the exam and what purpose they serve.

- Alternatives analysis selects a corrective action or a combination of corrective and preventive actions to implement
- Cost-benefit analysis is a financial tool used to determine the benefits provided by a project against its costs. You can use it to determine the best corrective action when it comes to cost factors in a project that deviates from the plan.
- Earned value analysis provides project managers with a more integrated perspective on scope, schedule, and cost performance
- Root cause analysis helps identify the main cause or causes of a problem
- Trend analysis helps forecast future performance based on past results
- Variance analysis reviews the differences between planned and actual performance.

Teams often use these techniques to consider and evaluate different options, approaches and paths that the project could take in executing the project work to meet the requirements and goals of the project.

2. How to handle change requests

When we analyzed the types of PMP exam questions students most get wrong on their mock exams, 24% of them related to project integration management.

Whether it's the people, the processes or the business environment related to integration, this is definitely a topic where students struggle.

Handling change requests is one of those topics.

Why people get it wrong
Understanding the first step in the process of handling change requests is typically the hardest part for a PMP aspirant.

Our team had an extensive debate on the subject of change requests and the sequence of steps involved in this process, because the *PMBOK® Guide* doesn't have a great explanation of the detailed process.

What you can do to get it right
After some late night and heated deliberations (as you can imagine, a team of certified project managers has strong opinions!), we concluded that the first thing that should be done when a change is requested on a project is the physical (or digital) creation of the change request form. In other words, someone has to submit a change request. Without that, there is nothing for the team, the change control board or any other stakeholder to evaluate – and this is in line with the guidance in the *PMBOK® Guide*.

After the change request is submitted, evaluated, and the alternatives discussed, a decision should be made as to whether to approve, reject, or defer the change. If the change is approved, it should be implemented. Finally, the implementation should be verified to ensure the change was implemented as approved.

Students often forget that submitting a change request should always be the first step.

3. The best tools to measure project progress
After integration management, the topic that causes the most headaches is scheduling. Whether you are in an agile team or a predictive environment, you still need to create a schedule and there are so many ways to do it.

Why people get it wrong
Questions on scheduling techniques are difficult because there are so many variables. Take this question, for example:

You are leading a complex project with a schedule baseline that cannot be modified due to external constraints. The scope, however, is flexible. The project deliverables are produced by three development teams that work independently from one another. The teams manage their workflow using Kanban. Which of the following is the most effective tool for you to use to measure the project's progress?

There are three teams involved. You know they are using Kanban but each team is working separately, although the delivery date is fixed. From the myriad of options, how do you choose which is the best approach?

What you can do to get it right
Most situational questions need you to take the approach of spotting which is the best out of the available responses. The possible answers to this question are:

- Burndown chart
- Burnup chart
- Cumulative flow diagram
- Feature chart

If you understand what benefit each of these tools brings to the project manager, it's easier to identify the correct answer.

- A burndown chart measures progress at a team level but wouldn't be helpful in this case.
- A burnup chart is the same: helpful for each of the teams to use to measure their progress but not useful to measure the progress of this particular project. Each team will set their own units of measure which makes it hard for the project manager to build a meaningful project level burndown or burnup chart.
- A cumulative flow diagram is designed to breakdown work in progress across a Kanban board rather than measure the project's progress.

That leaves the feature chart. A feature chart can provide information about the features that have been completed, the features remaining, and the total number of features, independent of story points assigned to each feature. Additionally, the feature chart can provide a visualization for the rate at which features are being developed.

This is the best response to the question, given the scenario.

4. The stages of team performance
The Tuckman ladder is one of the models used to describe stages of team development. The model includes five stages:

1. Forming
2. Storming
3. Norming
4. Performing
5. Adjourning

While it is safe to say that most teams go through all five stages, some may get stuck in a particular stage or even regress (go back) to an earlier stage. On the other hand, projects with team members who worked together in the past might skip a stage.

Why people get it wrong

Questions about team development can be challenging because they require you to read into the scenario and make judgments about how the team is working together.

In particular, students often get confused between the forming and storming stages.

What you can do to get it right

Read the question thoroughly and look at the language used to describe the team.

Team effectiveness is at its lowest level during the forming and storming stages. The main difference between the two is that while during the forming stage, the team members work independently, in storming, they begin to try to work together.

In the storming stage, the environment is characterized by a high degree of conflict and a lack of collaboration among the team members. As the team members begin to work together and trust each other, in other words, the relationships between the team members normalize (thus the name of the next stage, norming), the degree of team effectiveness increases.

Teams that successfully go through the norming stage would eventually reach the performing stage, which is the highest level of team development. In the performing stage, the team functions as a well-organized unit, and the team effectiveness is at its highest.

Adjourning happens at the end of the project, as the team disbands once the project is complete.

5. The difference between parametric and analogous estimating

This topic was raised by one of our expert PMP trainers, Antje Lehmann-Benz, from her knowledge of what students get wrong in the classroom.

"Even after discussing and explaining, people tend to confuse parametric and analogous estimating," she says. "This is just such a recurring issue in training."

Why people get it wrong

If you've struggled with this, you are not alone! "The confusion is not so much the fault of the people who are confused," Antje explains. "It's because of how the *PMBOK® Guide* distinguishes between them."

What you can do to get it right

The term 'analogous estimating' is confusing because there is no non-analogous estimating. Any estimate always uses reference points (analogies) to predict future performance, because if you don't do that you are basically guessing.

Parametric estimating is a form of analogy because it uses past data to inform the estimate.

Think of analogous estimating as a broad, top-down approach to using past projects to estimate current and future work. It's an educated guess based on what you know happened in the past.

Parametric estimating is based on data that can be scaled: the old adage of if it takes one person one hour to dig a hole, it will take one person two hours to dig two holes. You can extrapolate the estimate based on known data points.

6. How to calculate expected monetary value (EMV)

This is another one that comes up in our online PMP training classroom sessions, flagged by our team of expert trainers. Expected monetary value (EMV) is a statistical technique that calculates the probable financial results of events.

Why people get it wrong

EMV is not like the other formulas you'll find in your study materials. It represents the financial gain or loss that will result when an event occurs. The output of this formula is monetary value that represents the expected gain or loss of an event should it come to be.

What you can do to get it right

The formula for EMV is:

EMV = Probability * Impact in currency.

There isn't an easy trick to getting this right: you simply have to memorize the formula. Remember that you need to have the probability of the event in order to work it out. For instance: If it rains, we will lose $200. There is a 25% chance that it will rain, therefore the EMV is: 0.25 * $200 = $50.

7. How to start a project

Questions about the beginning of a project are also on the 'extra difficult' list. Project initiation seems to trip up students time and time again!

Why people get it wrong

It's possible to learn the steps for correctly initiating a project, so it's likely people get these questions wrong because what they see in real life doesn't follow established best practice! Another reason is because the beginning of a project changes depending on the size of the project.

In large projects, a project management team normally does the majority of the planning, and the remainder of the project team is brought on when the initial planning is complete, at the start of the development or execution phase.

Scenario-based questions ask you to make the right choice from a range of possible answers, and that's another reason why people trip up: several options could be correct.

Take this question, for example:

An organization is considering a product development project. A needs assessment and the business case have already been completed. A management team wants the product to begin delivering business value as soon as possible. As part of pre-project work, what should be done next?

What you can do to get it right

Think about how projects should be started and also look for clues in the scenario. In this question, the scenario stipulates that pre-project work is still being performed and that the needs assessment and business case have already been completed.

The only other project artifact that might be developed as part of pre-project work would be the benefits management plan. The benefits management plan should include target benefits and a timeframe for realizing the benefits.

The question also talks about delivering value as soon as possible. The minimum marketable features (MMF) represent the bare minimum of features and functionality that are required to release a product to derive business value.

Therefore, the release of the MMF would be the earliest that business value could be derived from the project. Choose the answer that most closely links to the MMF and benefits management plan.

8. What goes into a WBS

The work breakdown structure (WBS) may be composed of control accounts, planning packages, and work packages. So why do questions on scope trip up so many students?

Why people get it wrong

Work packages are the easy part of the WBS. However, the other aspects may be included. It's important to understand the other components, even if you don't have practical experience of using them on your real-life projects.

Sometimes test takers try to create or look for a work sequence in the WBS. A WBS is a structured breakdown, but it does not give you a sequence for performing the work. Students may be selecting the answer that includes sequencing.

Another potential reason why questions about WBS are tricky is that students draw on their own experiences when answering them – in fact, this is a risk for many questions. A WBS needs to be developed based on the individual needs of a project. The student may be ignoring the keywords in the question and then select the answer based on a past WBS they created themselves for their own projects.

Watch out for the level of detail; it's possible to get this question wrong by choosing the answer with the wrong level of detail. A WBS needs to have 'just the right amount' of detail in it. Too much and too little is unnecessary and will lead to you selecting the wrong answer. Read the question to determine what level you need.

A final reason why students sometimes get WBS questions wrong is that they forget that 'project management work' should be included in the WBS as well. A WBS includes 100% of the work that you need to deliver on the project, including the PM deliverables (schedules, reports, etc.).

What you can do to get it right

Understand the different project artifacts and what they represent. When you know how they are used, it's easier to see how they relate to project scope management and the WBS – if, indeed, they do at all.

Here are some common aspects of project scope management and their definitions.

Control account	A point where scope, budget, cost, and schedule are integrated and compared to earned value for performance measurement
Planning package	A component below the control account with known work content but without detailed schedule activities
Activity list	A documented tabulation of schedule activities that shows their description, identifier, and scope of the work
Work package	The work defined at the lowest level for which cost and duration are estimated and managed

Control accounts, planning packages and activity lists are all important, but they don't make up part of the WBS.

9. How to manage risk in agile sprints

Only about a quarter of the hardest PMP questions draw on the Agile Practice Guide, but the topic of risk management spans both agile and predictive workplaces.

Let's take a look at this question:

The first iteration of an agile project is about to begin. The sponsor gathers the team, the scrum master, the product owner, and other project stakeholders for the kick-off meeting. The sponsor emphasizes the need to identify and respond to the project risks as early in the project as possible and at the minimal cost. What is the best way for the meeting participants to implement the sponsor's request?

Why people get it wrong

This is an example of a question where a couple of words can make all the difference to the answer. Let's take a look at three incorrect answers and see if you can spot why they are wrong.

Answer choice	This is wrong because...
The project stakeholders should conduct risk-based spikes in each sprint.	Risk-based spikes can be conducted to address project risks. However, these efforts are carried out by the project team members, rather than stakeholders (read the answer choice carefully!). Additionally, risk-based spikes are performed as needed, rather than in each sprint.
The product owner and the sponsor should prioritize high-risk user stories.	It is true that the high-risk user stories should be properly prioritized to address risk early in the project. However, this activity is performed by the product owner in collaboration with the team and other relevant stakeholders (including the sponsor, if needed), but not exclusively with the sponsor.
The team should implement pair programming with the scrum master.	Pair programming is an agile software development practice in which two team members develop software code in pairs, periodically switching roles and reviewing the work of each other in real-time. This practice helps reduce risks as errors are detected quickly. The scrum master, however, is not involved in pair programming. This one should be easy to eliminate.

What you can do to get it right

Read the answer choices carefully. A few words like 'sponsor' or 'each' can make the difference between the choice being a viable answer or an incorrect response.

The correct answer to this question draws on agile principles: if in doubt, go back to agile principles to guide you to an appropriate response.

In agile projects, the risk is addressed in each sprint as part of backlog prioritization. Once the sprint is over, the stakeholders review the product increment and provide their feedback. This course of action allows the agile teams to increase review frequency with appropriate stakeholders, thus resulting in early risk mitigation at a minimal cost.

10. How to close a project
The end of a project also causes challenges for students on their exam.

Why people get it wrong
The Close Project or Phase process includes a step that confuses many students: it's the part where you confirm the delivery or formal acceptance of deliverables.

Students often forget that measuring stakeholder satisfaction is part of the project closure.

Another area of project closure that catches people out is what happens when a project is terminated prematurely. In our data, we see students often selecting the 'throw in the towel' option: they choose the answer about stopping work instantly. However, the correct choice (if one is provided) would be to begin the Close Project or Phase process.

What you can do to get it right
There are a lot of steps in closing out a project, even if the project is terminated early. Regardless of the reason for stopping the work, you want to make sure that the closedown process is structured and professional.

Remember that deliverables need to be formally accepted by the relevant stakeholders. Once that has happened, don't make the mistake of assuming the project is complete and the project team can be released. There are still tasks associated with the administrative closure of the project. Some of these tasks may require some of the team members, so releasing the team might be premature.

PART TWO

Test Yourself

Are you ready to put your knowledge to the test? In this section of the book, you'll find 50 tricky PMP questions and the corresponding answers. Your challenge is to find the correct answer for each question.

> There is a downloadable answer sheet available for you at **https://www.pm-exam-simulator.com/50answers**.
>
> Print that off to use to record your answers, and then you can test yourself again in the future if you would like to.

Remember, these are the most challenging questions: the questions that most of our students get wrong in The PM Exam Simulator (https://www.pm-exam-simulator.com), so it is quite likely you'll find them difficult. That's the point!

Are you ready for your first question? Let's go!

Q1 Question 1

You have just been assigned to an upcoming agile project. As part of pre-project work, you review all of the organization's policies and procedures regarding compliance. You realize that only some of them may be applicable to your project.

What should you do first?

- [ ] A) Switch the project management approach from agile to traditional
- [ ] B) Incorporate all compliance policies and procedures in the implementation strategy
- [ ] C) Ensure compliance activities are included in the project schedule baseline
- [ ] D) Classify the compliance categories to determine the expenditure of project resources

Q2 Question 2

A project manager is in the process of developing the schedule management plan. Since the customer has expressed the need for early and frequent delivery of business value, the project manager elects to incorporate iterative scheduling with a backlog.

Which of the following will need to be addressed in the schedule management plan for this project? (Choose three.)

- [ ] A) Using a Kanban board to pull work from the backlog when resources become available
- [ ] B) Accounting for rolling wave planning based on an adaptive life cycle
- [ ] C) Documenting the requirements in the form of user stories
- [ ] D) Decomposing work packages into an activity list during initial project planning
- [ ] E) Prioritizing and refining the user stories in the project backlog

Q3 Question 3

You have been requested to fill in for a scrum master during the upcoming sprint. As you get yourself familiar with the project team members, you are glad to see that they understand the project goals and their roles and responsibilities, there are no conflicts in the team, and each team member works independently. However, the velocity is low.

Based on your observations, where is the team on the Tuckman ladder?

(On the real PMP exam you may be asked to provide your answer by clicking the correct area in the image. But in this book, we are asking you to select the answer below.)

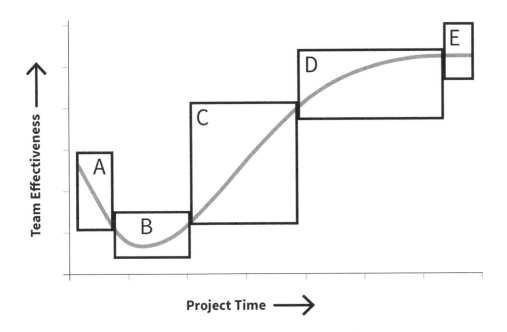

- ☐ A) A
- ☐ B) B
- ☐ C) C
- ☐ D) D
- ☐ E) E

Question 4

You meet with your team to determine the life cycle for your project. After analyzing the best way to define and manage requirements, develop deliverables, handle changes, control risk and cost, and engage key stakeholders, the decision is made to select a hybrid life cycle.

With the project life cycle selected, how will the product be delivered?

- ☐ A) As subsets of the overall product
- ☐ B) As a single final product at the end of the project
- ☐ C) As work packages of the WBS
- ☐ D) As product increments based on customer's value

Question 5

Midway into project execution, a stakeholder approaches the project manager requesting a change to one of the project deliverables.

In what order should the project manager take the following steps to process the stakeholder's request? (In your exam, on a question like this you would be asked to drag and drop the items from right to left. In this book, please arrange the answer choices in the correct order.)

Answer choices	Answers
Step one	
Step two	
Step three	
Step four	
Step five	
Step six	

- Look for alternatives
- Make a decision
- Verify the implementation
- Submit a change request
- Implement the change
- Evaluate the change

Question 6

During project planning, the project team rigorously defined the project scope. During project execution, a senior engineer calls the project manager and suggests a simpler and more efficient design that could benefit the project.

What should the project manager do next?

- ☐ A) Nothing, no changes are needed since the project scope was rigorously defined
- ☐ B) Discuss the change with the project sponsor
- ☐ C) Evaluate the impact of the proposed change on the project constraints
- ☐ D) Ask that the engineer submit a change request

Question 7

You and your team are in the process of determining, documenting, and managing stakeholder needs and requirements to meet project objectives.

As part of this process, you would use all of the following tools or techniques except for:

- [ ] A) Document analysis
- [ ] B) Alternatives analysis
- [ ] C) Nominal group technique
- [ ] D) Multicriteria decision analysis

Question 8

You are leading a large and complex project. Due to the size and complexity of the project, you have decided that a project management team will perform most of the planning, and the remainder of the project team will be brought on when the initial planning is complete.

In this scenario, when is the best time to conduct the project kick-off meeting?

- [ ] A) As project execution begins
- [ ] B) Shortly after project initiation
- [ ] C) As part of pre-project work
- [ ] D) During initial project planning

Question 9

A project manager is leading a meeting with key stakeholders to update them on the progress of the project as well as address any questions or concerns of the stakeholders. In order to capture relevant information from the meeting, the project manager assigns a project team member to be the meeting scribe. The meeting is a success with enthusiastic participation among the stakeholders.

With the meeting concluded, what should be done with the meeting minutes?

- [ ] A) Captured in the meeting minutes register
- [ ] B) Added to the communications management plan
- [ ] C) Recorded in the lessons learned register
- [ ] D) Documented in the organizational process assets

Q10

Question 10

You have tasked the project team with identifying and documenting the specific activities required to produce a key project deliverable. The team's work will result in schedule activities that can provide a basis for estimating, scheduling, executing, monitoring and controlling the project work.

Which of the following tools and techniques is least likely to be used during this process?

- [ ] A) Decomposition
- [ ] B) Rolling wave planning
- [ ] C) Expert judgment
- [ ] D) Leads and lags

Q11

Question 11

During a sprint planning session, the development team is arguing over the user stories to be included in the sprint goal. Everyone is actively listening as each team member is given an opportunity to express their concerns, and the scrum master does not feel the need to intervene.

What level of conflict did the scrum master most likely identify in this situation?

- [ ] A) The storming stage
- [ ] B) A crusade
- [ ] C) The performing stage
- [ ] D) A problem to solve

Q12

Question 12

To mitigate recent labor issues and reduce their risk in the future, senior executives are considering alternatives for automating production. One executive is not in favor of using automation at all; a second executive suggests adding some basic automation, and yet another one is in favor of automating the entire production line.

Which of the following is the least likely option to be included in the business case?

- [ ] A) Do nothing
- [ ] B) Do more than the minimum work possible to address the problem
- [ ] C) Do the minimum work possible to address the problem
- [ ] D) Do less than the minimum work possible to address the problem

Question 13

A project manager creates a procurement statement of work (SOW) from the project scope baseline. The scope of the SOW, however, is not yet well defined, therefore the project manager decides to contract with a vendor to provide an agile team of programmers. The contract is structured with fixed-price increments based on user stories.

How might the project manager verify that the vendor has met the contractual obligations?

- [ ] A) Wait until the team completes the development of all user stories specified in the SOW
- [ ] B) Request the product owner to approve or reject user stories during a sprint review
- [ ] C) Validate the user stories as soon as they are completed at any point during a sprint
- [ ] D) Conduct a procurement audit with the vendor each time a sprint retrospective is held

Question 14

For the third consecutive time, at the end of each iteration, a software application developed by the team fails during the Control Quality process conducted by the quality assurance (QA) department. This situation causes rework for the product and a delay in the project schedule. The project manager wants to reduce the feedback loop to the shortest possible interval.

What is the best course of action for the project manager?

- [ ] A) Shorten the iteration length
- [ ] B) Reduce the size of the user stories
- [ ] C) Revise the schedule baseline
- [ ] D) Suggest pair programming to the team

Question 15

The project manager has just completed gathering and documenting the requirements for a construction project in accordance with the scope management plan. Using decomposition along with other relevant tools and techniques, the project manager needs to create the scope baseline.

Based on this information, in what order will the following tasks need to be completed? (In your exam, on a question like this you would be asked to drag and drop the items from right to left. In this book, please arrange the answer choices in the correct order.)

Answer choices	Answers
Step one	
Step two	
Step three	
Step four	
Step five	
Step six	
(Not applicable)	

- Determine the planning packages of the WBS
- Create the project scope statement
- Finalize the WBS dictionary
- Identify control accounts for the WBS
- Document the work package cost estimates
- Develop the work packages for the WBS
- Gain approval for the scope baseline

Q16 Question 16

A project manager has been assigned to a heavily-regulated drug development project that will use traditional waterfall phases combined with agile methodologies. Currently, the project manager is conducting a communication requirements analysis as part of the development of a communications management plan.

What is the best strategy to address the communication needs of this hybrid project?

- [ ] A) Determine directions of influence of each project stakeholder and include the results in the communications management plan
- [ ] B) Ensure that only the regulatory compliance elements of the project are included in the communications management plan
- [ ] C) Develop the requirements list specific to the waterfall phases and use regulatory obligations as overarching requirements for all phases
- [ ] D) A communications management plan is not necessary when some of the project phases are executed using an agile approach.

Question 17

A traditionally managed project is using Scrum to develop the project deliverables. The agile release plan calls for the recently completed MVP to be deployed into production. However, the quality assurance (QA) department rejects the MVP, stating that the department's policies and procedures do not address the implementation of interim deliverables.

After recording the issue on the impediment board, what should the project manager do next?

- [ ] A) Submit a change request to update the quality control measurements
- [ ] B) Request the project sponsor's help with obtaining the necessary approvals
- [ ] C) Ignore the QA department's opinion and release the MVP as scheduled
- [ ] D) Ask the project team to deliver a feature-complete product before deployment

Question 18

You have joined a project in which requirements are elaborated at several intervals during delivery, and the delivery is divided into subsets of the overall product. Change is incorporated at periodic intervals, and risk and cost are controlled by progressively elaborating the plans with new information. Key stakeholders are regularly involved.

What development approach is used on your project?

- [ ] A) Agile
- [ ] B) Predictive
- [ ] C) Hybrid
- [ ] D) Periodic

Question 19

To promote continuous improvement, your organization uses a methodology that involves defining the objectives and scope of the project, measuring to obtain data, analyzing the collected data to find the root causes, improving by developing a solution, and controlling by evaluating the implemented solution.

What quality improvement method is your organization using?

- [ ] A) Total quality management (TQM)
- [ ] B) Six Sigma
- [ ] C) Quality function deployment (QFD)
- [ ] D) Deming's PDCA cycle

Q20

Question 20

Project stakeholders meet to discuss the threat of a severe staff shortage due to a potential union workers' strike that might take place during project execution. With various response strategies on the table, the stakeholders want to make a decision as to how to address the issue should the threat occur.

What response strategy will the stakeholders be using while deciding to implement one of the following decisions? (In your exam, on a question like this you would be asked to drag and drop the items from right to left. In this book, please arrange the answer choices in the correct order.)

Answer choices	Answers
Cancel the project	
Outsource staffing	
Automate processes	
Hire reserve workers	
Delegate to management	

- Escalate
- Avoid
- Mitigate
- Transfer
- Accept

Q21

Question 21

You are in charge of a large project to install 5G internet hubs across your city. Although most of the project variables are clear and can be managed using the waterfall approach, technical aspects are not fully defined and will be elaborated as the project progresses. The sponsor requests that project information will be communicated more frequently and quickly.

To address the sponsor's request, you will use all of the following, except:

- [ ] A) Holding frequent team checkpoints
- [ ] B) Conducting regular stakeholder reviews
- [ ] C) Implementing information radiators
- [ ] D) Communicating project status weekly

Question 22

As product increments are developed and then deployed at customer premises, the customer initiates new requirements, submits changes, and reports defects. The requirements, changes, and defects are reviewed by the CCB comprised of the project manager, product owner, and team, and prioritized for the upcoming iterations. The scope baseline is updated accordingly.

How should the work on the new requirements, changes, and defects be carried out?

- [ ] A) As specified in the requirements traceability matrix
- [ ] B) According to the organizational process assets
- [ ] C) Using a single-list-of-work-and-changes approach
- [ ] D) By implementing enterprise environmental factors

Question 23

A large multi-year manufacturing project relies on traditional and agile methods to manage the vast project complexities and external dependencies. Due to those external dependencies, there are many challenges that cannot be addressed or budgeted for in the two-week iteration cycle.

How should the team address the longer-term budget challenges?

- [ ] A) Facilitate a quarterly review of the budget and explore potential future budget challenges
- [ ] B) Slowly inject more budgetary constraints and track the budget challenges that these constraints cause
- [ ] C) Steadily burn down the budget with every iteration and mitigate budget challenges
- [ ] D) Re-evaluate the budget after every iteration and add identified budget challenges to the risk register

Question 24

A research project is characterized by high variability and uncertainty. The project scope is only known at a high level, so the WBS will have to be progressively elaborated throughout the project's life cycle. As the project manager estimates the team resources and various roles required for the project, she realizes that estimation is going to be a challenging task.

What is the best course of action for the project manager?

- [ ] A) Adopt three-point estimating as a technique to determine the number of team members required for each role

☐ B) Identify specific individuals to assign the roles of an agile coach, product owner, and cross-functional team members

☐ C) Use analogous estimating to estimate the team resource requirements and include in the resource requirements document

☐ D) Estimate team resources at the activity level and then aggregate to develop estimates for work packages, control accounts, and summary project levels

Question 25

An organization is considering a product development project. A needs assessment and the business case have already been completed.
A management team wants the product to begin delivering business value as soon as possible.

As part of pre-project work, what should be done next?

☐ A) Developing a WBS that is decomposed to a level to support an MVP in the first release of the product under development

☐ B) Creating a list of objectives and reasons for project initiation and including them in the project business documents

☐ C) Recording the need to release an MMF as part of the timeframe for benefits realization in the benefits management plan

☐ D) Documenting an incremental life cycle in the project charter as the approach needed to deliver business value quickly

Question 26

You plan a project where you need several external contractors to complete the project deliverables. In past projects, internal developers have had disruptive personality conflicts with contractors. Therefore, before making any long-term commitments, you want to ensure that the contractors are a good fit for your corporate culture and will work well with the internal team.

What is your best course of action?

☐ A) Send potential contractors to team building workshops

☐ B) Conduct a trial engagement with several potential contractors for initial deliverables

☐ C) Cover the team charter with the contractors before engaging their services

☐ D) Organize a meet and greet with potential contractors and the development team

Question 27

During project execution, a change request is submitted to include a new set of high-priority requirements to the product. The change requires an increase in the project scope and budget. The change request is approved, and the project manager updates the document that will be used in the Control Scope process to detect any deviation in the agreed-upon scope.

Which of the following documents did the project manager update?

- [ ] A) Requirements documentation
- [ ] B) Requirements traceability matrix
- [ ] C) Scope management plan
- [ ] D) Configuration management plan

Question 28

A conflict between the project manager and the team has been going for a while. The conflict negatively impacts the team's morale and jeopardizes the project's goals. To find a suitable resolution technique, the project manager maps the desire to satisfy the concerns of the parties on the chart below. Based on the map, the project manager decides to smooth the conflict.

Where did the project manager most likely map the desire to satisfy the team members' concerns vs. the desire to satisfy his/her own concerns?

(On the real PMP exam you may be asked to provide your answer by clicking the correct area in the image. But here in this book, we are asking you to select the answer below.)

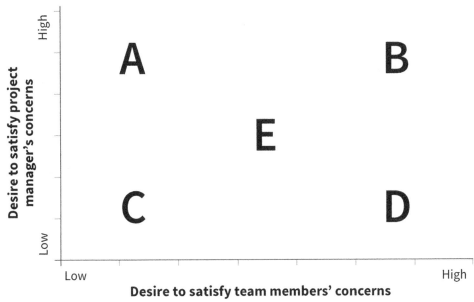

- ☐ A) A
- ☐ B) B
- ☐ C) C
- ☐ D) D
- ☐ E) E

Q29 Question 29

As the project manager, you are in the process of developing a draft of a document that authorizes a new software development project. You have reviewed the agreements and both business documents.

What else should be done as part of this process?

- ☐ A) Identify stakeholders and prepare the stakeholder register
- ☐ B) Study the governance functions and processes to provide guidance and decision making
- ☐ C) Update the business documents to correct any errors
- ☐ D) Review the benefits management plan

Q30 Question 30

During project execution, the project manager learns of a new government regulation that will impact her commercial building construction project. Specifically, regulatory compliance will now require the addition of a redundant fire suppression system. This risk had been identified during initial project planning, and appropriate contingency reserves were allocated. The project manager submits a change request, which is subsequently approved.

Which of the following project artifacts will most likely be updated as a result of this regulatory change? (Choose four.)

- ☐ A) Cost baseline
- ☐ B) Scope baseline
- ☐ C) Risk register
- ☐ D) Change management plan
- ☐ E) Activity list
- ☐ F) Configuration management plan
- ☐ G) Change log

Question 31

An agile team is using a Kanban board to manage their workflow. The work in progress limits (WIP) are indicated at the header of each column. The team reviews the board during the daily standup meeting to coordinate their activities for the day.

Which of the following actions might the team consider taking? (Choose three.)

To Do (eight)	Development (four)	Integration (two)	Testing (two)	Acceptance (three)	Deploy to Production
User story 21	User story 19	User story 17	User story 15	User story 11	User story 1
User story 22	User story 20	User story 18	User story 16	User story 12	User story 2
User story 23				User story 13	User story 3
User story 24					User story 4
User story 25					User story 5
User story 26					User story 6
User story 27					User story 7
User story 28					User story 8
					User story 9
					User story 10

- [ ] A) Add another user story from the backlog to the 'To Do' column
- [ ] B) Swap a user story from the 'To Do' column with a user story from the backlog
- [ ] C) Pull an item from the 'To Do' column to begin development work
- [ ] D) Assuming integration for user story 17 is complete, begin its testing
- [ ] E) Deploy user story 16 to production since that column does not have WIP limits
- [ ] F) Gain acceptance for user story 13 and deploy it to production

Question 32

You and your project team have just completed defining the scope for your project and are now in the process of decomposing the scope statement to create the work breakdown structure (WBS). Some of the deliverables will be produced later in the project and cannot be entirely decomposed at this time.

When you have completed the process of creating the WBS, your scope baseline will include which of the following components?

- [ ] A) Project scope statement, WBS, and activity attributes
- [ ] B) Project scope statement, WBS, WBS dictionary, and activity list
- [ ] C) Project scope statement, activity list, and activity attributes
- [ ] D) Project scope statement, work packages, and planning packages

Question 33

You are leading a complex project with a schedule baseline that cannot be modified due to external constraints. The scope, however, is flexible. The project deliverables are produced by three development teams that work independently from one another. The teams manage their workflow using Kanban.

Which of the following is the most effective tool for you to use to measure the project's progress?

- [ ] A) Feature chart
- [ ] B) Burndown chart
- [ ] C) Burnup chart
- [ ] D) Cumulative flow diagram

Question 34

To develop an appropriate approach and plan for project communication activities, the project manager identifies several project artifacts.

What relevant information can the project manager obtain from each project artifact to begin the process? (In your exam, on a question like this you would be asked to drag and drop the items from right to left. In this book, please arrange the answer choices in the correct order.)

Answer choices	Answers
Project charter	
Stakeholder register	
Enterprise environmental factors	
Organizational process assets	
Project management plan	

- Communications activities with stakeholders
- The list of key project stakeholders
- Management strategies to engage stakeholders
- Geographic distribution of resources
- Policies and procedures for social media

Question 35

A project sponsor tells the project manager that stakeholder expectations and risk thresholds have not been addressed by a particular document. Project planning cannot begin until the sponsor approves this document.

What might the project manager have neglected?

- ☐ A) Review of organizational process assets
- ☐ B) Consideration of enterprise environmental factors
- ☐ C) Development of a risk management plan
- ☐ D) Creation of the risk register

Question 36

A project is plagued by various issues, such as a deteriorating team performance, cost and schedule overruns, defective deliverables, etc. The project manager is struggling to monitor and control the work and decides to use some of the data analysis techniques to identify the issues and determine the best course of action.

How can the project manager use the following techniques to identify the various issues impacting this project? (In your exam, on a question like this you would be asked to drag and drop the items from right to left. In this book, please arrange the answer choices in the correct order.)

Answer choices	Answers
Corrective actions for better performance	
Corrective actions regarding the cost	
Integrated perspective on project performance	
Identify the main reason for problems	
Forecast performance based on results	
Compare planned and actual performance	
(Not applicable)	

- Earned value analysis
- Trend analysis
- Variance analysis
- Business analysis
- Root cause analysis
- Alternatives analysis
- Cost-benefit analysis

Q37

Question 37

All the technical work on a project has been completed, and the product has been transitioned to a support team.

What should the project manager do before the project can be closed?

- [ ] A) Issue a quality report
- [ ] B) Validate the scope
- [ ] C) Close the contracts
- [ ] D) Measure stakeholder satisfaction

Q38

Question 38

During a software development project, developers spent two days to repair a defect that was found a day earlier. The deployment team then spent another day to deploy the fix at the customer premises.

Which of the following does this four-day period represent?

- [ ] A) Lead time
- [ ] B) Actual time
- [ ] C) Cycle time
- [ ] D) Response time

Q39

Question 39

You are managing a project team that has recently been expanded by new team members working remotely from another country. Their roles have been outlined to form a preliminary team charter. Nevertheless, you have noticed a considerable lack of acceptance of cultural differences in the team, resulting in frequent conflicts.

Which of the following techniques could help you in this situation?
(Choose three.)

- [ ] A) Focus groups
- [ ] B) Role definition
- [ ] C) Ground rules
- [ ] D) Ability tests
- [ ] E) Meetings

Question 40

During iteration planning, an agile coach wants to ensure that her development team has an easy way of organizing their work as well as a visual representation at a glance of the work remaining to be completed in an iteration.

Which of the following tools is best for the agile coach to use to accomplish his goals?

- ☐ A) A burndown chart
- ☐ B) A task board
- ☐ C) A burnup chart
- ☐ D) A glance chart

Question 41

A project manager is nearing the end of a product development project for a large consumer goods manufacturer. Several vendors produced key deliverables for the project, and there are no open claims. The project manager is now carrying out all of the activities associated with project closure and is following all project management best practices.

Which of the following tasks should the project manager perform?

- ☐ A) Close procurements with the vendors
- ☐ B) Formally sign off the project deliverables
- ☐ C) Update the enterprise environmental factors
- ☐ D) Update the organizational process assets

Question 42

During a daily standup meeting, the project manager goes from one team member to another questioning each one on the work they have accomplished and reprimanding them for the slow progress the team has made so far. The meeting lasts for almost an hour and turns into a status meeting.

What should the project manager do differently to avoid the next standup meeting turning into a status meeting?

- ☐ A) Use a timer configured to alarm 30 minutes after the start of the meeting
- ☐ B) Switch the development life cycle from adaptive to predictive
- ☐ C) Ask a team member to facilitate the standup instead of the project manager
- ☐ D) Only focus on issues that represent roadblocks and impediments to progress

Question 43

To create initial user stories, the product owner is facilitating a story writing workshop with the team and project stakeholders.

What is the main focus of this workshop?

- [ ] A) To create as many user stories as possible
- [ ] B) To create user stories for the first iteration
- [ ] C) To refine user stories in the product backlog
- [ ] D) To re-prioritize user stories for the first release

Question 44

A scrum master is leading a drug development project for a large pharmaceutical company. She is concerned about the impact of potential changes in the business environment including regulatory, technological, geopolitical, and marketplace, that can impact the product backlog and the project as a whole.

What sequence of steps should the scrum master take to address these changes to the project? (In your exam, on a question like this you would be asked to drag and drop the items from right to left. In this book, please arrange the answer choices in the correct order.)

Answer choices	Answers
Step one	
Step two	
Step three	
Step four	
Step five	

- Assess the impact of the changes on the backlog
- Revise the backlog based on the suggested options
- Identify changes to the external business environment
- Review the environment for any additional changes
- Recommend options for backlog adjustment to changes

Question 45

An agile coach wants to ensure that expectations between him and the team members are properly set. The coach meets with the team and emphasizes that he will adhere to the servant leadership approach while working with the team members.

What should the team expect the least from the agile coach?

☐ A) Continuously reminding the team about the purpose of the project
☐ B) Encouraging the team to create an environment where everyone can succeed
☐ C) Focusing on results rather than on a perfect agile development process
☐ D) Providing feedback on the product increment developed by the team

Question 46

As the project progresses and deliverables are being produced, the project manager revisits the stakeholder engagement plan to determine what refinements can be made to the plan to improve stakeholder engagement.

Among the project documents, which will be the most influential to the project management process being performed? (Choose three.)

☐ A) Stakeholder register
☐ B) Risk register
☐ C) Resource management plan
☐ D) Stakeholder engagement assessment matrix
☐ E) Issue log

Question 47

You are facilitating a risk workshop with your project team to discuss, evaluate, and prioritize previously identified project risks based on the probability and impact of each risk. During the meeting, a key stakeholder proposes that as part of the analysis, the team consider other characteristics of risk beyond just probability and impact.

Which of the following is the least likely characteristic proposed by the stakeholder:

☐ A) Dormancy
☐ B) Propinquity
☐ C) Manageability
☐ D) Sensitivity

Q48

Question 48

An agile team uses a Kanban board to manage their workflow. As part of continuous improvement efforts, the team reviews the process they have been using so far to develop the project deliverables. With the help of a software project management tool, the team creates a cumulative flow diagram, as shown below. Today is Day 8 of the project.

Where is the bottleneck in the process?

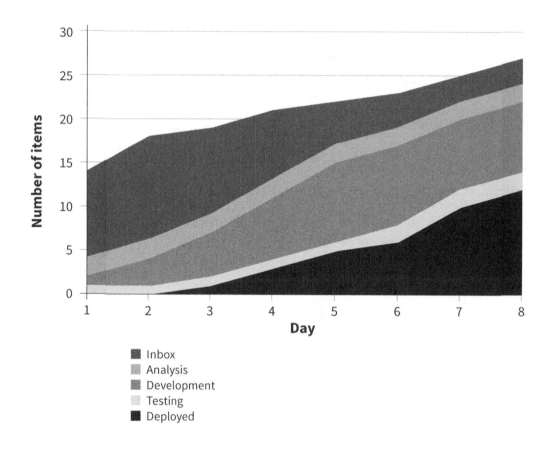

- Inbox
- Analysis
- Development
- Testing
- Deployed

- [ ] A) Analysis
- [ ] B) Development
- [ ] C) Testing
- [ ] D) Deployment

Question 49

Q49

Defects have been found in some of the project deliverables. The change request to repair the defects has been submitted and approved, and the deliverables repaired.

What should the project manager do next?

- [ ] A) Invite the customer to validate scope
- [ ] B) Conduct the approved change requests review
- [ ] C) Perform the Control Scope process
- [ ] D) Request the team to carry out a root cause analysis

Question 50

Q50

The first iteration of an agile project is about to begin. The sponsor gathers the team, the agile coach, the product owner, and other project stakeholders for the kick-off meeting. The sponsor emphasizes the need to identify and respond to the project risks as early in the project as possible and at a minimal cost.

What is the best way for the meeting participants to implement the sponsor's request?

- [ ] A) The team and stakeholders should frequently review product increments.
- [ ] B) The project stakeholders should conduct risk-based spikes in each sprint.
- [ ] C) The product owner and the sponsor should prioritize high-risk user stories.
- [ ] D) The team should implement pair programming with the agile coach.

PART THREE

Check Your Answers

You've made it through the questions! In this part of the book, you'll check your answers and dive deep into both the wrong choices and the correct choices.

There is a lot of information in this section, along with references for further reading about a topic and tips for how to answer similar types of questions on your exam day.

You're probably desperate to know how you did on the questions in Part 2, so you might want to skim this section to mark your work. The correct answers are highlighted in bold underneath the question, or you can use the filled in answer sheet which is downloadable here: **https://www.pm-exam-simulator.com/50answers**.

Then, go back and read through the explanations and notes for each question. I suggest you work through a few questions at a time as there is a lot to take in. Build some time into your study plan to review your answers and keep coming back to this section on a regular basis.

You'll probably want to take notes and refer to your reference materials to deepen your knowledge of each topic.

Ready to see how you did with the questions? Get your answer sheet and check your work!

A1 Question 1: Answer

You have just been assigned to an upcoming agile project. As part of pre-project work, you review all of the organization's policies and procedures regarding compliance. You realize that only some of them may be applicable to your project.

What should you do first?

- A) Switch the project management approach from agile to traditional
- B) Incorporate all compliance policies and procedures in the implementation strategy
- C) Ensure compliance activities are included in the project schedule baseline
- ✔ **D) Classify the compliance categories to determine the expenditure of project resources**

All answers:

- A) Switch the project management approach from agile to traditional
Incorrect. The selection of a project management framework should be based upon the needs of the project rather than simply compliance activities. Compliance can be effectively addressed by any project management framework.

- B) Incorporate all compliance policies and procedures in the implementation strategy
Incorrect. According to the scenario, only some of the organization's policies and procedures regarding compliance will be applicable to the project. There is no reason to develop strategies for the policies and procedures that do not apply to the project. This action would be inconsistent with the agile principle of maximizing the amount of work not done.

- C) Ensure compliance activities are included in the project schedule baseline
Incorrect. A schedule baseline is typically used on projects led by a predictive project management approach, while the scenario describes an agile project.

- ✔ **D) Classify the compliance categories to determine the expenditure of project resources**
Correct. Classifying the compliance categories that have been captured in the organization's policies and procedures may be helpful in differentiating those that require the expenditure of resources and those that do not.

Explanation:
The scenario describes a situation where only some compliance-related policies and procedures for an agile project will be applicable. One of the principles outlined in the Agile Manifesto states, "Simplicity – the art of maximizing the amount of work not done – is essential." Compliance activities represent overhead, which does not directly provide value. In keeping with an agile mindset, the project manager should minimize the overhead and only include those compliance activities that are necessary.

Classifying the compliance categories is one of the tasks associated with the Business Environment domain of the Project Management Professional (PMP)® Examination Content Outline. Classifying the compliance categories that have been captured in the organization's policies and procedures may be helpful in differentiating those that require the expenditure of resources and those that do not. For example, the organization may have specific guidelines for complying with union rules and activities. However, if the project underway will not have union involvement, then that entire compliance category can be disregarded.

References:
Agile Practice Guide – First Edition, Project Management Institute Inc, 2018, Page(s) 8-9

Agile Project Management, Second Edition, Jim Highsmith, 2009, Delivery versus Compliance

Project Management Professional (PMP)® Examination Content Outline, Project Management Institute Inc., June 2019, Domain 3, Task 1

Did you get it right?

The biggest reason why this one is very tough is that the correct choice – answer D – doesn't sound exactly correct, largely because of its use of the phrase: "Classify the compliance categories."

In the ECO, Task 1 in Domain III, 'Plan and Manage Compliance' says "Classify compliance categories" as the second bullet, which is almost identical to the phrase in the answers. However, test takers are still at risk of getting this question wrong. Here are some reasons why.

- Not every test taker understands that they need to read the ECO very carefully and know it really well, which means applying it in their studying, and being able to apply it on the test.
- The phrase in the ECO is short and doesn't say enough about what actually needs to happen.

What we believe it means is that the project manager should do a high-level classification first, selecting the areas of compliance that are pertinent to the project, and then drilling-down to specifically fulfil the necessary policies and procedures. In other words, for this question, tailoring the organization's compliance policies to your project.

The incorrect answers make this question even harder.

Switching to waterfall is pretty obviously the wrong choice, but some test takers might panic at the word 'compliance' and think they better get away from agile and back to waterfall, to increase their chances of being in compliance.

Choice B sounds correct except for the word 'all' which makes it incorrect. The question says only some of the compliance policies and procedures have been determined necessary. However, some test takers still might choose this answer over D, because D is a somewhat vague statement.

Choice C sounds good except for the phrase 'schedule baseline'. If it said 'backlog' (signifying agile, as per the question) it would be more tempting.

As you plan and carry out your studies, remember to use the ECO and review it very carefully. Apply it to your studying to the point that you will be able to keep it in mind during the test.

Also remember to be on the lookout for whether a scenario is waterfall or agile, as that can drive the correct choice of tools, ceremonies, etc. and make it easier for you to choose the correct answer.

Question 2: Answer

A project manager is in the process of developing the schedule management plan. Since the customer has expressed the need for early and frequent delivery of business value, the project manager elects to incorporate iterative scheduling with a backlog.

Which of the following will need to be addressed in the schedule management plan for this project? (Choose three.)

A) Using a Kanban board to pull work from the backlog when resources become available

☑ **B) Accounting for rolling wave planning based on an adaptive life cycle**

☑ **C) Documenting the requirements in the form of user stories**

D) Decomposing work packages into an activity list during initial project planning

☑ **E) Prioritizing and refining the user stories in the project backlog**

All answers:

A) Using a Kanban board to pull work from the backlog when resources become available
Incorrect. This answer choice describes on-demand scheduling rather than Iterative scheduling with a backlog. On-demand scheduling does not rely on a specific schedule and, therefore, would not ensure early and frequent delivery of business value as requested by the customer.

☑ **B) Accounting for rolling wave planning based on an adaptive life cycle**

Correct. Iterative scheduling with a backlog is a form of rolling wave planning based on adaptive life cycles, which will need to be accounted for as part of project schedule management planning.

☑ **C) Documenting the requirements in the form of user stories**

Correct. When incorporating a project backlog, the features that comprise the project scope are typically expressed in the form of user stories. The project backlog will include additional work items that have to be completed as part of the project.

D) Decomposing work packages into an activity list during initial project planning

Incorrect. When incorporating agile methodologies, the project scope is progressively elaborated. Work packages represent the lowest level of the work breakdown structure (WBS). Since the project scope will be progressively elaborated, a fully decomposed WBS will not be available to create an activity list during initial project planning.

☑ **E) Prioritizing and refining the user stories in the project backlog**

Correct. When using iterative scheduling with a backlog, the user stories in the project backlog will need to be refined and prioritized with each iteration. Note, 'project backlog' is not a typo. Both, product backlog and project backlog, are valid terms. The former includes user stories related to the development of the product itself, while the latter has a broader meaning and, on top of the product-related items, may include project-wide activities, for example, deploying the product and training the customer who will then maintain and operate the product after it has been deployed.

Explanation:
The scenario describes a project that will incorporate agile practices within an overarching project management plan, including a schedule management plan, which makes this a hybrid project. Among the trends and emerging practices in schedule management is the use of iterative scheduling with a backlog, which is a form of rolling wave planning based on adaptive life cycles.

When using this approach, the project scope will be progressively elaborated throughout the course of the project. With each iteration, the project scope, as captured in the project backlog in the form of user stories, will be refined and prioritized during iteration planning.

The correct answer choices represent elements that will need to be incorporated into the schedule management plan to accommodate this scheduling method. The incorrect answer choices represent other scheduling methods.

References:

A Guide to the Project Management Body of Knowledge, (*PMBOK® Guide*) – Sixth Edition, Project Management Institute Inc., 2017, Page(s) 177

Agile Practice Guide – First Edition, Project Management Institute Inc, 2018, Page(s) 52

Exploring Scrum: The Fundamentals, 2nd Edition, Dan Rawsthorne with Doug Shimp, 2013, The Backlog

Did you get it right?

This is a tough question because you have to know four flavors of project management to get it right:

- Waterfall
- Scrum
- Kanban
- Hybrid

and then identify which apply to the scenario.

It's also takes a lot more brain work to pick out three correct answers instead of simply choosing one.

Make sure you are very familiar with the top agile methods and study

- The Agile Practice Guide
- The Agile Manifesto and the 12 Principles
- The Scrum Guide.

Look for clues in questions like this to help you work out which methods are being used. For example, in this question the two big clues are these phrases:

- 'Schedule Management Plan' indicates waterfall or hybrid
- 'Early and frequent delivery of business value... iterative scheduling with a backlog' indicates agile or hybrid.

Let's look at some more phrases from the question to help uncover the correct answers.

There is nothing about Kanban's 'pull' suggested in this question, so A needs to be rejected as not pertinent to the scenario.

'Decomposing work stories into an activity list' is clearly waterfall, so, again, not pertinent to the scenario.

That leaves us with three correct choices. Rolling wave planning is not explicitly mentioned in the question, but it does fit the terms 'iterative scheduling' and 'frequent delivery' which are both mentioned in the question. What's a little tricky about this choice is that rolling wave planning is not necessarily tied to agile, or to hybrid. It has long been part of predictive approaches, so some test takers may find that confusing.

'User stories' definitely suggests agile, and often Scrum, but Scrum is not mentioned. This choice indirectly fits the scenario. This forces the test taker to consider this one to see if it's one of the best three out of five, since the question is asking for three – but it's not a definite until all five are evaluated.

Prioritizing and refining the user stories in the project backlog very much fits the scenario, and again leads us to a correct answer.

Question 3: Answer

You have been requested to fill in for a scrum master during the upcoming sprint. As you get yourself familiar with the project team members, you are glad to see that they understand the project goals and their roles and responsibilities, there are no conflicts in the team, and each team member works independently. However, the velocity is low.

Based on your observations, where is the team on the Tuckman ladder?

(On the real PMP exam you may be asked to provide your answer by clicking the correct area in the image. But in this book, we are asking you to select the answer below.)

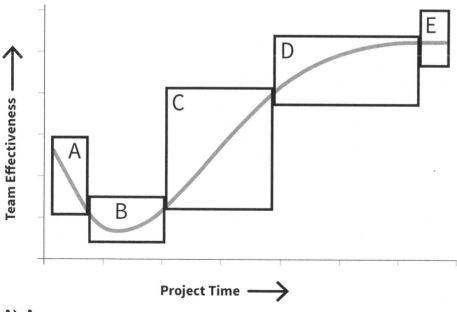

☑ A) A
B) B
C) C
D) D
E) E

All answers:

✓ **A) A**

Correct. Area A represents the forming phase of the team development model. In this phase, the team members meet and learn about the project and their formal roles and responsibilities. Team members tend to be independent and not as open. The scenario closely matches this description, making forming the best answer to the question asked.

B) B

Incorrect. Area B represents the storming phase of team development. During this phase, the team begins to address the project work, technical decisions, and the project management approach. However, the storming phase is characterized by a high degree of conflict. If team members are not collaborative, the environment can become counterproductive, resulting in low team effectiveness. This description does not match the one provided in the scenario.

C) C

Incorrect. Area C represents the norming stage of the team development model. In this phase, team members begin to work together and adjust their work habits and behavior to support the team. The team members learn to trust each other. In the scenario, the team members work independently, making this choice an incorrect answer.

D) D

Incorrect. Area D represents the performing stage of the team development model, where the team's performance is at its highest level. Teams that reach this level of development, function as well-organized units. The team members are interdependent and work through issues smoothly and effectively. In the scenario, the velocity is low. Therefore, the team is not in the performing stage.

E) E

Incorrect. Area E represents the adjourning stage of the team development model. This is the last stage of the Tuckman ladder, in which the team completes the work and moves on from the project. The scenario implies the team is still working together (carrying out one of the sprints), suggesting adjourning is an incorrect answer.

Explanation:

The Tuckman ladder is one of the models used to describe stages of team development. This model is typically referred to by project management practitioners as part of the Develop Team process. The model includes five stages: forming, storming, norming, performing, and adjourning. While it is safe to say that most teams go through all five stages, some may get stuck in a particular stage or even regress (go back) to an earlier stage.

On the other hand, projects with team members who worked together in the past might skip a stage. Each stage is distinguished by different dynamics among the team members resulting in various levels of team effectiveness. Team effectiveness is at its lowest level during the forming and storming stages. The main difference between the two is that while during the forming stage, the team members work independently, in storming, they begin to try to work together.

In the storming stage, the environment is characterized by a high degree of conflict and a lack of collaboration among the team members. As the team members begin to work together and trust each other, in other words, the relationships between the team members normalize (thus the name of the next stage, norming), the degree of team effectiveness increases. Teams that successfully go through the norming stage would eventually reach the performing stage, which is the highest level of team development. In the performing stage, the team function as a well-organized unit, and the team effectiveness is at its highest.

The role of a project manager (or scrum master, agile coach, servant leader, facilitator, etc.) is also different during different team development stages. In the forming stage, the project leader should set goals, provide direction, and help establish ground rules. During the storming stage, which is typically the most difficult one, the project leader should facilitate conversations between the team members, ensure that the team members listen to and respect each other, and help resolve conflicts. The norming stage allows the project leader to loosen their grip, let the team resolve issues and conflicts, and step in as needed to ensure the team keeps moving in the right direction.

When the team reaches the performing stage, the project leader typically acts as an observer, stepping in only when a decision needs to be made at a higher level within the organization. And finally, during the adjourning stage, which coincides with the end of the project, a good project leader ensures the team is recognized for their achievement in project completion, the success is celebrated, and lessons learned are captured.

References:
A Guide to the Project Management Body of Knowledge, (*PMBOK® Guide*) – Sixth Edition, Project Management Institute Inc., 2017, Page(s) 338

https://www.projectmanagement.com/blog-post/15192/The-Five-Stages-of-Team-Development-and-the-Role-of-the-Project-Manager

https://www.projectmanagement.com/wikis/609109/Tuckman-model--Tuckman-s-stages-of-group-development-

Did you get it right?

Here are some reasons why test takers get this question wrong.

- They don't know the Tuckman Model well enough.
- They read the scenario quickly so they don't fully understand what is being asked.
- They are caught out by the term 'low velocity', which does not necessarily point to the Forming phase. The team could have low velocity while Storming, Norming or Performing.
- They overlook the key phrase: "and each team member works independently" which is hidden in the middle of the scenario. This phrase is the one that is key in making the correct choice because team members would almost always be working together, not independently, in the Performing stage. However, their real-life experience may tell them that on some projects each team member does work largely independently, which could lead them to conclude that the Performing stage is the correct response.

Under the time-pressure of the test and the hurry to get to the point of the question, you could read this question and select Performing thinking that the team was already formed, was past Storming because there are no conflicts, and getting work done, albeit at low velocity.

Getting this answer right depends on reading the full question and understanding the Tuckman Model, so let's dive into that a little.

More on Tuckman

A variation of the Tuckman Model came out later that added another phase called the High-Performing stage. This stage specifically addressed this point: that a team could move from Performing (low velocity) to High-Performing. It also specified that not all teams reach the High-Performing phase.

If the test taker is thinking of the advanced model that includes the High-Performing phase, they might choose Performing as the response because the team could be in the Performing phase and not have high-velocity, which many teams don't have on all projects.

Another phrase that is a subtle indicator that points to Forming over Performing is the phrase: "There are no conflicts on the team."

That might sound good to the test taker, who might logically think, "The team must be past the Storming stage since there are no conflicts," but as books about the Tuckman Model make clear:

- Conflict is healthy
- There usually is healthy conflict in the Performing Stage (and in Norming and possibly Adjourning).

The fact that there are no conflicts is more suggestive of being in the Forming stage, before the team have started to truly work together.

Question 4: Answer

You meet with your team to determine the life cycle for your project. After analyzing the best way to define and manage requirements, develop deliverables, handle changes, control risk and cost, and engage key stakeholders, the decision is made to select a hybrid life cycle.

With the project life cycle selected, how will the product be delivered?

✓ **A) As subsets of the overall product**
   B) As a single final product at the end of the project
   C) As work packages of the WBS
   D) As product increments based on customer's value

All answers:

✓ **A) As subsets of the overall product**
Correct. Hybrid life cycles, like the one described in the scenario, combine the delivery methods of both predictive and agile methods. Predictive projects deliver a single final product at the end of the project. Agile projects deliver product increments frequently. Therefore, delivering the overall product in subsets best describes the hybrid project life cycle.

B) As a single final product at the end of the project
Incorrect. Delivering a single final product at the end of the project is a characteristic of a predictive project life cycle, while, according to the scenario, a hybrid life cycle has been selected for the current project,

C) As work packages of the WBS
Incorrect. A work package is the work defined at the lowest level of the work breakdown structure (WBS), for which cost and duration are estimated and managed. While a WBS can be used on both predictive and hybrid projects, work packages, on their own, as their definition implies, do not typically represent deliverable items.

D) As product increments based on customer's value
Incorrect. Delivering working product increments based on their value to the customer is the pinnacle of the agile delivery methods. While this delivery approach can be applied on both agile and hybrid projects, another answer choice better describes the way the product is delivered on projects carried out using a hybrid life cycle.

Explanation:

Predictive and agile project life cycles differ from one another in several aspects. One of them is the way the project product, service, or result is delivered. Predictive projects develop plans up-front and deliver only a single final product (service or result) at the end of the project. Agile projects, on the other hand, deliver working product increments as frequently as possible based on the highest value to the customer. Everything in between is defined as a hybrid delivery.

With hybrid project life cycles, the product can be divided into subsets, which are delivered at either pre-defined intervals or as soon as the subsets are completed. Therefore, of the choices provided, with the hybrid life cycle selected, delivering the result of the project as subsets of the final product constitutes the best answer to the question asked.

Reference:

A Guide to the Project Management Body of Knowledge, (*PMBOK® Guide*) – Sixth Edition, Project Management Institute Inc., 2017, Page(s) 666

Did you get it right?

This is a very tough question because choices A and D are very similar. The main difference between A and D is that D includes 'based on customer's value' which is clearly a signpost towards agile.

Here are some reasons why test takers get this question wrong.

- They think hybrid means 'using largely Agile methods, while still delivering one main deliverable at the end like waterfall.' Choice B looks very much like waterfall and therefore is the most obviously incorrect. However, some test takers may choose it because they misunderstand what hybrid is.
- They think that hybrid could allow for using work packages like in waterfall, but fulfilling them with agile methods, like sprints. This may happen if the term 'work package' is used in your workplace to mean 'tasks we have to get done' instead of its true, specific, meaning.

It seems very likely that you will face questions testing exactly the issue at the heart of this question: is it hybrid or agile?

And as with the correct answer here, some variation of the concept of 'based on customer's value' could very likely be the differentiator. Make sure you understand what hybrid environments look like and how projects work within them so you can identify a hybrid scenario.

Question 5: Answer

A5

Midway into project execution, a stakeholder approaches the project manager requesting a change to one of the project deliverables.

In what order should the project manager take the following steps to process the stakeholder's request? (In your exam, on a question like this you would be asked to drag and drop the items from right to left. In this book, please arrange the answer choices in the correct order.)

Answer choices	Answers
Step one	
Step two	
Step three	
Step four	
Step five	
Step six	

- Look for alternatives 3
- Make a decision 4
- Verify the implementation
- Submit a change request 1
- Implement the change 5
- Evaluate the change 2

Answers:

Answer choices	Answers (correct order)
Step one	**Submit a change request**
Step two	**Evaluate the change**
Step three	**Look for alternatives**
Step four	**Make a decision**
Step five	**Implement the change**
Step six	**Verify the implementation**

Explanation:

Understanding the first step in the process of handling change requests is typically the most difficult thing for a PMP aspirant. Our team had an extensive debate on the subject of change requests and the sequence of steps involved in this process. The reason being is that the *PMBOK® Guide* does not do a good job of explaining the exact process in detail. We have discussed the sequence of steps among our team of certified project management professionals and have concluded that the first thing that should be done when a change is requested on a project is the physical (or digital) creation of the change request form, a document if you wish.

In other words, submitting a change request, for example, filling out a form, is the first thing that should be done when a change is requested on the project. Otherwise, on what basis would a project manager, the project team, the change control board (CCB), and other relevant stakeholders spend time evaluating a request that is not even documented?

While the *PMBOK® Guide* does not explicitly specify the above sequence, it does imply that a change request should first be documented and only then evaluated. On page 120, the *PMBOK® Guide* reads, "Change control meetings are held with a change control board (CCB) that is responsible for meeting and reviewing the change requests and approving, rejecting, or deferring change requests. Most changes will have some sort of impact on time, cost, resources, or risks. Assessing the impact of the changes is an essential part of the meeting. Alternatives to the requested changes may also be discussed and proposed. Finally, the decision is communicated to the request owner or group." Therefore, the fact the CCB meets to review change requests and evaluate their impact on project constraints implies the change requests have already been submitted prior to the meeting.

After the change request is submitted, evaluated, and the alternatives discussed, a decision should be made as to whether to approve, reject, or defer the change. If the change is approved, it should be implemented. Finally, the implementation should be verified to ensure the change was implemented as approved.

Reference:
A Guide to the Project Management Body of Knowledge, (*PMBOK® Guide*) – Sixth Edition, Project Management Institute Inc., 2017, Page(s) 120, 305

Did you get it right?
The biggest reason test takers get this wrong is they reverse the order of the first two correct choices.

The correct order here is:

- A) Submit the change request
- B) Evaluate the change

However, many test takers likely will put evaluate the change first. In the real world, many project managers probably do evaluate the change to some extent before submitting the change, or before helping the stakeholder create a change request and submit it. There is definitely a real-world argument for not submitting a change request blindly without the project manager at least giving it a cursory look first. Equally, some project managers may believe it is part of their role to go the extra mile and provide some evaluation and insight into a change request before sending it to the CCB.

Finally, some project managers may do this 'because they are the project manager and it's their project, and they know best,' so they want to guide the change to the CCB in the right direction.

The lesson here is to once again, put away your real-world experience and answer the question based on your study materials.

Question 6: Answer

A6

During project planning, the project team rigorously defined the project scope. During project execution, a senior engineer calls the project manager and suggests a simpler and more efficient design that could benefit the project.

What should the project manager do next?

- A) Nothing, no changes are needed since the project scope was rigorously defined
- B) Discuss the change with the project sponsor
- C) Evaluate the impact of the proposed change on the project constraints
- ✓ **D) Ask that the engineer submit a change request**

All answers:

- A) Nothing, no changes are needed since the project scope was rigorously defined
  Incorrect. Regardless of how much time was spent during project planning and how well the scope was defined, expecting no changes on a project would be naive thinking. Changes are normal as project work is performed.

- B) Discuss the change with the project sponsor
  Incorrect. Although discussing the change with the project sponsor may be required at some point, this action is unlikely to be the next step for the project manager to take.

C) Evaluate the impact of the proposed change on the project constraints
Incorrect. While the impact of the proposed change on the project constraints should be evaluated, the change request should be created first to capture the details and rationale of the engineer's proposed change request. Otherwise, on what basis would the project manager and the team spend time evaluating a request that is not even documented?

✓ **D) Ask that the engineer submit a change request**
Correct. A change request is a document to record a change that may affect the competing project constraints. Given that this change was proposed in a phone call, the change request will also provide a means to capture the details required to evaluate the impact of the change to the project.

Explanation:
A change request is a document to record an adjustment to project scope, schedule, cost, etc. Changes may include corrective action, preventive action, or defect repair, among others. The engineer is proposing what she believes to be a valid design change which can be further evaluated by the change control board.

Although changes may be initiated verbally, they should be recorded in written form and entered into the change management and/or configuration management system. Of the available choices, asking the engineer to create and submit a change request is what the project manager should do next, and is, therefore, the best answer to the question asked.

You might argue that evaluating the change should come before submitting the change request. We had an extensive debate on the subject of change requests in general and on this question in particular. That's because the *PMBOK® Guide* does not do a good job in explaining the exact process in detail.

We have discussed this process among our team of certified project management professionals and have concluded that the first thing that should be done when a change is requested on a project is the physical creation of the change request, a document if you wish, filling out a form. Otherwise, on what basis would a project manager and the project team spend time evaluating a request that is not even documented?

Reference:
A Guide to the Project Management Body of Knowledge, *(PMBOK® Guide)* – Sixth Edition, Project Management Institute Inc., 2017, Page(s) 115

Did you get it right?

Here are some reasons why test takers sometimes get this question wrong.

- They feel that the scenario falls under gold plating because the deliverables are already being built and there is no bug. As there are always different ways to do things, they may feel that it's best to just keep going and finish the project as planned. Therefore, they jump to the 'do nothing' option because that suggests the team can avoid scope creep or gold plating the solution. However, the solution here is to submit a change request for consideration and not simply to ignore the engineer.
- They might evaluate the impact on project constraints in real-life as a first step.
- Not all projects in the real world have a change control board (CCB), even though it is a waterfall/predictive standard.
- They feel they should evaluate the change first against the project constraints before taking up the time of the CCB on a request they might not agree with themselves.
- They might feel that the engineer only sees the benefit of the change request but not the big picture and that it's the team and project manager's responsibility to consider the big picture first before submitting the request to the CCB.

More about change requests

The *PMBOK® Guide* clearly agrees with choice D (submit a formal change request). It states that:

> "Although changes may be initiated verbally, they should be recorded in written form and entered into the change management and/or configuration management system... Whenever a change request may impact any of the project baselines, a formal integrated change control process is always required."

This is a challenging topic as some of the PMP prep material presents slightly different approaches to the order of what to do. Option C is going to look better to some people. However, we always recommend going back to the *PMBOK® Guide* as your final arbitrator if you are in doubt, and it is very clear about this point.

Another thing that makes this question difficult is that it goes against the agile point of view. In agile, there is a heavy emphasis on the team making the decisions on their own. This question is an 'old school' perspective that is still valid for predictive approaches. Many project managers today are learning agile first, so this is going backwards in philosophy for them. We do it this way in agile, with the team taking responsibility for decisions and changes, but for this kind of test question, you have to know the predictive approach too, even if that is counter-intuitive to how agilists see it.

Let's look at some more phrases from the question to help uncover the correct answers.

There is nothing about Kanban's 'pull' suggested in this question, so A needs to be rejected as not pertinent to the scenario.

'Decomposing work stories into an activity list' is clearly waterfall, so, again, not pertinent to the scenario.

That leaves us with three correct choices. Rolling wave planning is not explicitly mentioned in the question, but it does fit the terms 'iterative scheduling' and 'frequent delivery' which are both mentioned in the question. What's a little tricky about this choice is that rolling wave planning is not necessarily tied to agile, or to hybrid. It has long been part of predictive approaches, so some test takers may find that confusing.

'User stories' definitely suggests agile, and often Scrum, but Scrum is not mentioned. This choice indirectly fits the scenario. This forces the test taker to consider this one to see if it's one of the best three out of five, since the question is asking for three – but it's not a definite until all five are evaluated.

Prioritizing and refining the user stories in the project backlog very much fits the scenario, and again leads us to a correct answer.

Question 7: Answer

You and your team are in the process of determining, documenting, and managing stakeholder needs and requirements to meet project objectives.

As part of this process, you would use all of the following tools or techniques except for:

A) Document analysis
☑ **B) Alternatives analysis**
C) Nominal group technique
D) Multicriteria decision analysis

All answers:

A) Document analysis
Incorrect. Document analysis can be used to elicit requirements by analyzing existing documentation and identifying information relevant to the requirements. It is a data analysis technique used during the Collect Requirements process implied by the scenario.

☑ B) Alternatives analysis

Correct. According to the scenario, the team is performing the Collect Requirements process. Alternatives analysis is not used during this process. Rather, this technique used in the Define Scope process to evaluate the requirements identified in the Collect Requirements process. Since the question is asking to find a technique which is not used during the Collect Requirements process, alternatives analysis is the best answer.

C) Nominal group technique

Incorrect. Nominal group technique is a structured form of brainstorming using a voting process to rank the generated ideas. This technique is an example of the interpersonal and team skills used during Collect Requirements, the process you are performing in the scenario described.

D) Multicriteria decision analysis

Incorrect. The scenario suggests the Collect Requirements process is underway. Multicriteria decision analysis is a technique that uses a matrix to provide a systematic approach to establishing criteria used to evaluate and rank ideas. It can be used in the Collect Requirements process as a decision-making technique.

Explanation:
Determining, documenting, and managing stakeholder needs and requirements to meet project objectives is the definition of the Collect Requirement process. The process provides the basis for defining the project scope. All of the answers, except alternatives analysis, are tools and techniques used when collecting requirements. Alternatives analysis is an example of the data analysis technique that can be used during the Define Scope process to select the final project requirements that will best meet the objectives identified in the project charter. Alternatives analysis is not a technique used in the Collect Requirements process and is, therefore, the best answer to the question asked.

Reference:
A Guide to the Project Management Body of Knowledge, (*PMBOK® Guide*) – Sixth Edition, Project Management Institute Inc., 2017, Page(s) 153, 142-147, 138

Did you get it right?

Here are some reasons why test takers get this very tough question wrong:

- They might have read the question quickly and missed a key point. It's another flavor of the 'backwards' question: whenever there's a question asking for "all of the following tools except for xxx", some people will miss that, and will look instead for the best tool for the process.

- They might not have heard of Nominal Group Technique so they won't recognize it as a valid solution for the scenario, and therefore they might choose it as the 'tool you would not use'.

- They may be confused between choices A, B, and D which all sound similar because they all end with the word analysis, compared to Nominal Group Technique, which is the only one that sounds different, and sounds like it is in its own category. They might guess that Nominal Group Technique is wrong because it sounds like the one that is different from the others.

- They might have rightly recognized that none of the incorrect answers sound particularly appropriate for Collecting Requirements.

- They might have realized that Alternatives Analysis is used in the Define Scope process, which is related and a follow-up to Collect Requirements. That might lead them to conclude it is not the correct choice because it is used in a related process.

- The question does not explicitly state you are Collecting Requirements – it does talk about 'determining, documenting, and managing stakeholder needs and requirements to meet project objectives' which might sound like the Define Scope process, and that process does use the tool of Alternatives Analysis.

- They might be confused by the use of the term 'stakeholder needs' in the question. While requirements certainly are part of stakeholder needs, the question mentions 'stakeholder needs and requirements'. They might start thinking about Stakeholder Analysis, Stakeholder Register, Stakeholder Engagement Plan, Stakeholder Engagement Assessment Matrix, etc. because the question gets them thinking about stakeholders, instead of just saying 'requirements' or 'collecting requirements' which would get them right away to thinking about what this question is going for.

More on Nominal Group Technique

The term 'nominal' is kind of abstract, and doesn't sound like what it means. It's also not a commonly-used word in English, so that also makes it harder.

PMP textbooks typically don't give it much coverage. Nominal group technique is defined in the *PMBOK® Guide* glossary but the description is too short and does not really explain it very well, compared to many other terms that are explained well in the glossary.

Another reason why nominal group technique is obscure is that agile has several similar methods like planning poker, affinity estimating and tee-shirt sizing techniques, all of which are probably much more common nowadays in the real world than nominal group technique, with the increasing popularity of agile.

It's a good idea to dig further into project management terms, especially the ones that you are not sure about. Just memorizing that the nominal group technique can be used for prioritizing or estimating is not enough for a scenario-based question like this one, where you need to know more about it.

Question 8: Answer

A8

You are leading a large and complex project. Due to the size and complexity of the project, you have decided that a project management team will perform most of the planning, and the remainder of the project team will be brought on when the initial planning is complete.

In this scenario, when is the best time to conduct the project kick-off meeting?

- ☑ **A) As project execution begins**
- B) Shortly after project initiation
- C) As part of pre-project work
- D) During initial project planning

All answers:

☑ **A) As project execution begins**

Correct. A project management team typically does the majority of the planning for a large project, and the remainder of the project team is brought on at the start of project execution. Therefore, the kick-off meeting for a large project should take place with processes in the Execution Process Group, making this the correct answer choice.

B) Shortly after project initiation

Incorrect. For small projects, the kick-off occurs shortly after initiation because the same team usually performs planning and execution. However, the question describes the project as being large and complex, making this an incorrect response.

C) As part of pre-project work

Incorrect. Pre-project work consists of creating the business case and benefits management plan before project initiation. The project is not authorized until the project charter has been approved. The kick-off meeting is held to communicate the start of the project, engage stakeholders, and gain commitment. Communicating the start of the project, engaging stakeholders, and gaining commitment to the project that has not been authorized does not make sense.

D) During initial project planning

Incorrect. The scenario states that only the project management team will be involved in the initial planning due to the size and complexity of the project. After initial planning is complete, the remainder of the project team is typically brought on to complete the rest of planning and start project execution. It is easier to gain commitment to the project from individuals who were part of its planning. Since one of the project kick-off meeting's goals is to gain commitment, initial project planning is not the best time for the project kick-off meeting to be conducted without having the remainder of the project team onboard.

Explanation:

The question describes a large and complex project. In large projects, a project management team normally does the majority of the planning, and the remainder of the project team is brought on when the initial planning is complete, at the start of the development/implementation.

In this instance, the kick-off meeting takes place with processes in the Execution Process Group. Therefore, of the choices provided, conducting the kick-off meeting during project execution is the best answer to the question asked.

Reference:

A Guide to the Project Management Body of Knowledge, (*PMBOK® Guide*) – Sixth Edition, Project Management Institute Inc., 2017, Page(s) 86

Did you get it right?

This is a very difficult question and you'll need to be extremely familiar with the *PMBOK® Guide* to get it right. Here is the main reason why test takers get it wrong.

- They might be drawing on their own experience of real-world projects, where kick-off meetings are held early in the planning stage. It makes sense intuitively that you wouldn't want to hold a kick-off meeting on a large project until the planning has been completed, but not all large teams are run that way.

The lesson here is to study the *PMBOK® Guide* carefully, because this question is right out of the book. It's also important to remember not to fall back blindly on your own work experience when answering questions.

However, that's not to say that your own experience (or the *PMBOK® Guide*) is wrong. Tailoring approaches is important. The approaches, processes, tools and techniques that are covered in the *PMBOK® Guide* are drawn from the experience of hundreds of certified professionals – they represent one way of doing things. To get this question right, you really need to follow what the *PMBOK® Guide* says, which may or may not be your way of working.

Question 9: Answer

A project manager is leading a meeting with key stakeholders to update them on the progress of the project as well as address any questions or concerns of the stakeholders. In order to capture relevant information from the meeting, the project manager assigns a project team member to be the meeting scribe. The meeting is a success with enthusiastic participation among the stakeholders.

With the meeting concluded, what should be done with the meeting minutes?

   A) Captured in the meeting minutes register
   B) Added to the communications management plan
   C) Recorded in the lessons learned register
☑ **D) Documented in the organizational process assets**

All answers:

   A) Captured in the meeting minutes register
       Incorrect. The 'meeting minutes register' is a term made-up for this question.

   B) Added to the communications management plan
       Incorrect. The communications management plan establishes how, when, and by whom information about the project will be administered and disseminated. The communications management plan does not serve as an archive for meeting notes.

   C) Recorded in the lessons learned register
       Incorrect. Lessons learned from the meeting may be captured in the lessons learned register for use later in the project. However, the question is not asking about where the knowledge gained from the meeting should be documented to improve the performance of the project. Rather, the question is simply asking about what should be done with the meeting minutes. Meeting minutes are considered project records and typically contain information that does not pertain to lessons learned. Recording the meeting minutes in the lessons learned register is unlikely to serve the purpose for which the lessons learned register was created.

☑ **D) Documented in the organizational process assets**
       Correct. The meeting minutes are project records that are considered an organizational process asset (OPA) and could be archived for future reference. Ideally, the meeting minutes should be shared with the

meeting participants and other stakeholders as necessary and then archived as part of the OPAs. However, this option is not provided. Therefore, of the choices given, updating the OPAs is the best answer to the question asked.

Explanation:

Organizational process assets updates are an output of the Manage Communications process described in the scenario. Organizational process assets may be updated with project records such as correspondence, memos, meeting minutes, project reports, presentations and other documents used on the project.

The meeting minutes are considered an organizational process asset and could be archived for future reference. Typically, after the meeting, the meeting minutes are distributed to the meeting participants and other project stakeholders as specified in the communications management plan. Then the meeting minutes can be archived as part of the OPAs update. However, an option that describes both of these steps is not provided as one of the answer choices.

Therefore, we have to select the answer that, among the choices given, best addresses the question asked. Among the choices provided, documenting the meeting minutes in the OPAs is the best answer to the question asked.

Reference:

A Guide to the Project Management Body of Knowledge, (*PMBOK® Guide*) – Sixth Edition, Project Management Institute Inc., 2017, Page(s) 388

Did you get it right?

Here are some reasons why test takers get this question wrong.

- They read the question and it seems easy, but then none of the four choices jump out as the right answer.
- They assume that this question is like so many other questions and is asking for either the first thing or the best thing a project manager should do. However, it is not asking for that. The primary action to take in this scenario is to distribute the meeting minutes to the stakeholders after the meeting. A later action is archiving.
- They may have chosen the meeting minutes register as it sounds consistent with waterfall approaches. However, there is no such artifact.
- They may have read the statement: "The meeting is a success with enthusiastic participation among the stakeholders," and concluded that there might be lessons to save in the lessons learned register because the meeting went so well, especially as none of the answers jump out as being obviously correct.

- They may have felt trapped into choosing choice B because none of the other answers looked correct to them. However, as minutes are not plans, this is incorrect.

You are not always looking for the first or best action to take on every question. Sometimes you have to settle for an action that may not be the first or the best, but is a valid response.

Another clue towards the correct answer is that PMI's preference is for project managers to archive documents in the OPAs for the next project. You may see this preference tested on more than one question.

Another useful rule of thumb to note is that you should assume that OPAs are available for use on projects, and that you are encouraged to look for those OPAs first, rather than just plunge ahead and sometimes re-invent the wheel, which is considered a wasteful, non-cost-effective way to work.

Question 10: Answer

A10

You have tasked the project team with identifying and documenting the specific activities required to produce a key project deliverable. The team's work will result in schedule activities that can provide a basis for estimating, scheduling, executing, monitoring and controlling the project work.

Which of the following tools and techniques is least likely to be used during this process?

- A) Decomposition
- B) Rolling wave planning
- C) Expert judgment
- ☑ **D) Leads and lags**

All answers:

A) Decomposition
   Incorrect. In the scenario, the project is in the Define Activities process. Decomposition, one of the tools and techniques in the Define Activities process, is used for dividing and subdividing deliverables into manageable parts. The question implies that the project team is using decomposition to identify and document the activities required to produce the deliverable. Therefore, decomposition is an incorrect answer.

B) Rolling wave planning
   Incorrect. Rolling wave planning is an iterative planning technique where work required in the near-term is planned in detail, and future

work is planned at a higher level. The project is in the Define Activities process, and while rolling wave planning is not explicitly mentioned in the scenario, it is a tool and technique that can be used in that process. Since the question asks which option is 'least likely' to be performed in the Define Activities process and rolling wave planning is a tool and technique of the process, rolling wave planning is not the best answer to the question asked.

C) Expert judgment
Incorrect. Expert judgment is judgment provided by individuals or groups that have knowledge and expertise in a subject matter. The scenario implies the project is in the Define Activities process. Even though the scenario does not mention expert judgment explicitly, it is a tool and technique of the Define Activities process, and 'could' be used as part of the process. Therefore, expert judgment is not the correct answer.

✓ **D) Leads and lags**
Correct. Leads and lags are a tool and technique used during the Sequence Activities process to produce a project schedule network diagram. Since the scenario describes the project as being in the Define Activities process, and leads and lags are used in the Sequence Activities process, it is unlikely that leads and lags would be used. Therefore, leads and lags is the correct answer.

Explanation:
In the scenario, the project is in the Define Activities process where work packages are decomposed into schedule activities that provide a basis for estimating, scheduling, executing, monitoring and controlling project work. Decomposition, rolling wave planning, and expert judgment are tools and techniques used in the Define Activities process.

The question is asking which of the answer choices is the 'least likely' to be performed during the Define Activities process. Since all of the answer choices except leads and lags are tools and techniques used in the Define Activities process, leads and lags is the correct answer.

Reference:
A Guide to the Project Management Body of Knowledge, (PMBOK® Guide) – Sixth Edition, Project Management Institute Inc., 2017, Page(s) 184-185, 192

Did you get it right?
Here are some reasons why test takers sometimes get this question wrong.

- They miss the fact that the question is asking for the 'least likely' response. Many questions ask you to choose the 'most likely' or 'best course of action' but you will see questions where the negative or least likely answer is required. Read the question carefully.

- They jump to the Develop Schedule process and start to picture a network diagram. Getting ahead of yourself will get you to the wrong answer here, because you might be thinking about leads and lags as part of planning the schedule. However, the question is really set in the Define Activities process, before the network diagram is first used in the Sequence Activities process, and long before leads and lags are applied to the network diagram in the Develop Schedule process.
- It's difficult for some people who don't follow the five sequence Schedule Planning steps in real life to realize that leads and lags are not applied in the *PMBOK® Guide* until the fifth of the five Schedule processes when using predictive approaches: the Develop Schedule process.
- The term 'leads' correctly implies 'early'. This can be a source of confusion for some test takers who think that they are used early when the schedule is first being built.
- They may not have grasped that some tools are used during several sequential activities and the network diagram is one of those. It is first built in the Sequence Activities process and then is elaborated during the two Schedule Planning processes that follow: Estimate Activity Durations and Develop Schedule. They may assume that everything to do with the network diagram is completed during the Sequence Activities process, including applying leads and lags.

The other two responses where people often make mistakes are incorrectly choosing decomposition or rolling wave planning. Let's look at why those might have looked right at first glance and why you shouldn't have chosen them.

More on decomposition
Many people first learn about decomposition as a key tool of the Create WBS process, as part of Scope Management before any the five Schedule Planning processes are carried out. From the experience of our trainers, I can tell you that a lot of people get it into their heads that there is one tool called decomposition used for creating work packages.

There are actually two types of decomposition:

- Scope decomposition is done first, where the work packages are created in the Create WBS process as part of Scope Management.
- Activity Decomposition is done a couple of steps later, in the Define Activities process as part of Schedule Management.

As the question doesn't specifically say 'scope' decomposition or 'activity' decomposition, you may have made the jump to scope management because it comes earlier in the *PMBOK® Guide* and you probably learned that meaning first.

Further adding to the confusion is that the term decomposition is also used in agile, and also in more than one way:

- Agile Decomposition: Breaking down features into epics into user stories, and then into tasks
- Agile Decomposition: Breaking down epics into Features into user stories, into tasks
- Agile Decomposition: Breaking down epics into user stories into tasks.

There's more on this in *PMI-ACP Exam Prep, 2nd Edition*, by Mike Griffiths (check out page 266).

More on rolling wave planning

Rolling wave planning is a valid tool here, but it wouldn't be the first tool people think about.

The question asks about documenting the creation of a specific deliverable. Rolling wave planning is a type of high-level planning. An example of where it is used would be planning Sprint #1 for Deliverable #1, Sprint #2 for Deliverable #2, and so on. It is somewhat counter-intuitive or abstract to think about rolling wave planning being used as a tool for the Define Activities process for just one deliverable. Even though it can be used for a complex deliverable like building a car, and the question is asking you to identify and document the specific activities required to produce a key project deliverable.

This would probably not be the typical use of an example of rolling wave planning, if you were looking at examples in a book or discussing them in a PMP prep class, even though it is a valid use.

A11 Question 11: Answer

During a sprint planning session, the development team is arguing over the user stories to be included in the sprint goal. Everyone is actively listening as each team member is given an opportunity to express their concerns, and the scrum master does not feel the need to intervene.

What level of conflict did the scrum master most likely identify in this situation?

- A) The storming stage
- B) A crusade
- C) The performing stage
- ☑ **D) A problem to solve**

All answers:

- A) The storming stage
  Incorrect. The storming stage represents one of the stages of the

Tuckman ladder model. The Tuckman ladder model addresses team development rather than levels of conflict, making this choice an incorrect answer.

B) A crusade

Incorrect. A crusade is the fourth of five levels of conflict. A crusade is characterized by team members splitting into entrenched factions, where people may be attacked for their affiliations rather than their ideas. However, in this scenario, the team is still working as a cohesive unit to reach an agreement.

C) The performing stage

Incorrect. The performing stage refers to the Tuckman ladder model of team development. In this stage, the team functions as a well-organized unit. The scenario indeed suggests the team is having a productive discussion and works through issues smoothly and effectively, implying the team is likely in the performing stage. However, the Tuckman ladder model addresses team development, rather than levels of conflict, as asked by the question.

☑ **D) A problem to solve**

Correct. A problem to solve represents a level one conflict out of five. The scenario indicates that the team may be in disagreement with each other, but they are actively listening to each other's concerns and confidently working toward a resolution without the need for intervention.

Explanation:

The scenario describes a situation where a development team is having a conflict over the sprint goal. All project teams will inevitably experience some level of conflict as the project progresses, and lower levels of conflict are considered healthy for the team. Speed Leas, the author of many books on conflict management, developed a model that categorized five levels of conflict, including a 'problem to solve', 'disagreement', 'contest', 'crusade', and finally 'world war'.

In this situation, the team members are working through the differing opinions in a respectful manner without any need for intervention. This situation is best described as a level one conflict, which is a 'problem to solve'. The incorrect answer choices represent either a stage of team development or a more extreme level of conflict where collaboration has been lost.

References:

A Guide to the Project Management Body of Knowledge, (*PMBOK® Guide*) – Sixth Edition, Project Management Institute Inc., 2017, Page(s) 61, 348, 338

Agile Practice Guide – First Edition, Project Management Institute Inc, 2018, Page(s) 33-35

Coaching Agile Teams, Lyssa Adkins, 2010, Coach as Conflict Manager

Did you get it right?

Here are some reasons why test takers get this tough question wrong.

- They might get confused between the two sources being tested: the Tuckman Ladder and the Five Stages of Conflict (which is lesser-known, but the source of the correct answer). Both have five components and they both involve conflict to some extent.
- They find it tricky to hold both models in their head at the same time for this question, especially as the five Tuckman stages do not have a one-to-one correspondence to the five stages of conflict.
- They are more familiar with Tuckman, so as soon as they see 'arguing' in the scenario, they jump to the Tuckman Storming phase.
- They might be thinking of another model, the Blanchard Model, that does have a one-to-one correspondence with the first four stages of the Tuckman Model.

It's really important to be able to identify what the question is asking about to be able to tackle questions like this.

Question 12: Answer

To mitigate recent labor issues and reduce their risk in the future, senior executives are considering alternatives for automating production. One executive is not in favor of using automation at all; a second executive suggests adding some basic automation, and yet another one is in favor of automating the entire production line.

Which of the following is the least likely option to be included in the business case?

- A) Do nothing
- B) Do more than the minimum work possible to address the problem
- C) Do the minimum work possible to address the problem
- ✓ **D) Do less than the minimum work possible to address the problem**

All answers:

- A) Do nothing
  Incorrect. Selecting this option results in the project not being authorized. This option is also referred to as the 'business as usual' option. Declining to authorize a desired or optional project is always a possibility.

- B) Do more than the minimum work possible to address the problem
  Incorrect. This option meets the minimum set of criteria and some or all of the other documented criteria. For example, in the scenario,

perhaps the company would authorize the project to replace the entire production line with a new automated system rather than just retrofit the existing production line.

C) Do the minimum work possible to address the problem
Incorrect. The minimum work possible meets the minimum set of criteria for the project. For this scenario, that might mean retrofitting the existing production line to incorporate automation.

✓ **D) Do less than the minimum work possible to address the problem**
Correct. Doing less than the minimum work possible to address the problem makes the least sense from a business perspective. Taking this option means that the company would expend company resources without receiving the benefits of the project. Why would the company authorize a project that does not produce the intended benefits?

Explanation:
A business case should include a set of options to be considered for addressing the business problem or opportunity. Options are alternative courses of action that may be taken by the organization. Doing less than the minimum work possible to address the problem makes the least sense from a business perspective. Taking this option means that the company would expend company resources without receiving the benefits of the project. Why would the company authorize a project that does not produce the intended benefits?

Reference:
A Guide to the Project Management Body of Knowledge, (*PMBOK® Guide*) – Sixth Edition, Project Management Institute Inc., 2017, Page(s) 31

Did you get it right?
This question is extremely tough, because it's a great example of double-negatives, but it is fair and representative of what you might get asked.

Here are some reasons why test takers get this question wrong.

- The big challenge here is the question is asking for a negative: Which of the four makes the least sense. By asking for the one that 'makes the least sense', some test takers will miss the word 'least' and they will get the question wrong because they will look for the one that makes the 'most' sense.
- As well as the challenge about correctly reading the question, the spirit of most of the PMP exam questions is to solve the problem and make the project succeed. So asking for the 'least sense' is going against that spirit: a lot of the questions are asking for the solution that makes the most sense.

- Then, making this all the tougher, the question becomes a test of double-negatives, which are always counter-intuitive and difficult by nature.
- They may choose the 'do nothing' option because it sounds negative, and as project managers are encouraged to be proactive, this sounds wrong. It is wrong, but we want to choose the answer the makes the least sense, so we have to look at the other choices to see if they are worse.
- They may choose the 'do the minimum work possible' option because project managers are encouraged to do their best, and the word 'minimum' sounds kind of negative. Plus, the word 'minimum' is part of MVP – Minimum Viable Product – which is sometimes a very much encouraged technique.

This question is a brain-teaser, and anyone could get a headache from it! Answer choice D is the clear winner as the worst of the four, so therefore it's the best choice.

A13 Question 13: Answer

A project manager creates a procurement statement of work (SOW) from the project scope baseline. The scope of the SOW, however, is not yet well defined, therefore the project manager decides to contract with a vendor to provide an agile team of programmers. The contract is structured with fixed-price increments based on user stories.

How might the project manager verify that the vendor has met the contractual obligations?

A) Wait until the team completes the development of all user stories specified in the SOW
☑ **B) Request the product owner to approve or reject user stories during a sprint review**
C) Validate the user stories as soon as they are completed at any point during a sprint
D) Conduct a procurement audit with the vendor each time a sprint retrospective is held

All answers:

A) Wait until the team completes the development of all user stories specified in the SOW
Incorrect. With a contract featuring fixed-price increments, the project scope (or the scope specified in the SOW in the scenario described) can be decomposed into fixed-price microdeliverables, such as user stories.

With this type of contract, there is no reason nor is this appropriate per agile best practices to wait until the entire project scope has been completed before approving the deliverables.

☑ **B) Request the product owner to approve or reject user stories during a sprint review**
Correct. During a sprint review, the development team demonstrates the product increment that was developed during the sprint. The product owner then has the responsibility for approving or rejecting the deliverables.

C) Validate the user stories as soon as they are completed at any point during a sprint
Incorrect. The use of sprints creates a cadence of predictable, timeboxed pre-agreed, consistent duration that aids with scheduling. Validating the user stories as soon as they are completed at any point in a sprint before the timebox is over, would interfere with the team's work, break the cadence, and negatively affect the project schedule, and may have other unintended consequences.

D) Conduct a procurement audit with the vendor each time a sprint retrospective is held
Incorrect. A procurement audit is a structured review of the procurement process between the buyer and seller (vendor). The emphasis is on the process of procurement rather than the deliverables produced by the vendor. Sprint retrospectives, on the other hand, are aimed to review the process the development team uses to carry out their work rather than review the procurement process.

Explanation:
The scenario describes a hybrid project where the scope is managed using a predictive project management approach (scope baseline), while the procurement portion of work is outsourced to a vendor who will use agile methods to develop the scope specified in the SOW. An agile framework is typically used when the project scope is not well understood at the start of the project (which is the case in the scenario described) and is progressively elaborated throughout project execution.

This situation creates special considerations when contracting with a vendor to supply developers. One method of addressing the issue is to use contract terms that include fixed-price increments. With this approach, the scope is decomposed into microdeliverables, such as user stories, and the vendor will be paid a fixed price for each of these microdeliverables.

In this scenario, the development team will complete the user stories determined during sprint planning. At the end of the sprint, during the sprint review, the development team will demonstrate the product increment that was developed during the sprint to the product owner and other relevant stakeholders. The product owner then has the authority and responsibility for approving or rejecting the deliverables.

References:

Agile Practice Guide – First Edition, Project Management Institute Inc, 2018, Page(s) 41, 55, 77

Agile Software Development: The Cooperative Game, Second Edition, Alistar Cockburn, 2007, Contracts

Exploring Scrum: The Fundamentals, Second Edition, Dan Rawsthorne with Doug Shimp, 2013, The Sprint

Did you get it right?

This question is a challenge because you need all three of the following:

- A good understanding of agile including sprints and sprint reviews.
- An understanding of hybrid approaches (waterfall/agile) to recognize that this is a hybrid scenario where you need to be thinking about an SOW (waterfall term) but also scrum sprints at the same time.
- An understanding of the role of a product owner in Scrum.

Two of the choices are obviously wrong, but choice C sounds a little like the XP best practice of continuous integration where all new code is implemented, for example, each night or several times a day.

Some test takers may choose C because the question might point them towards that as a valid agile practice to use in the scenario. However, the wording on the choice is that each story will be validated as soon as it is completed, which is not the way continuous integration is usually done.

More on statements of work

This question is additionally confusing because instead of 'SOW' (which is the commonly-used term), the question uses the term 'Procurement Statement Of Work (SOW)'.

This is a distractor because we use the term SOW all the time, and not with 'Procurement' in front of it. This makes you wonder if it's something else other than the kind of SOW we usually see on questions and on projects. And you'd be right.

Both SOW and Procurement SOW are defined separately in the *PMBOK® Guide* glossary. The Procurement SOW is the correct choice for dealing with a vendor.

However, most people in real life loosely use the single term 'SOW' whether they mean it as a Procurement SOW or for internal projects inside their company without a Vendor.

This is another example of a question where it's important to understand the terminology. Take the time to review the glossary and commit what's there to memory.

Question 14: Answer

A14

For the third consecutive time, at the end of each iteration, a software application developed by the team fails during the Control Quality process conducted by the quality assurance (QA) department. This situation causes rework for the product and a delay in the project schedule. The project manager wants to reduce the feedback loop to the shortest possible interval.

What is the best course of action for the project manager?

A) Shorten the iteration length
B) Reduce the size of the user stories
C) Revise the schedule baseline
☑ **D) Suggest pair programming to the team**

All answers:

A) Shorten the iteration length
Incorrect. While shortening the iteration length would allow the team to gain feedback from the QA department earlier in comparison to the current cadence, agile best practices discourage changing the iteration length in the middle of a project.

B) Reduce the size of the user stories
Incorrect. Since the testing is done at the end of each iteration, reducing the size of the user stories would not progress work items from development to testing quicker. The QA department would still have to wait until all the user stories in the iteration are completed whether the user stories are big, medium, or small. Additionally, it's up to the team, not the project manager, to determine whether a user story should be split.

C) Revise the schedule baseline
Incorrect. According to the scenario, there are already delays to the project schedule. Therefore, it is reasonable to assume that the schedule baseline will need to be revised. However, this action would not shorten the feedback loop, as requested by the question.

☑ D) Suggest pair programming to the team

Correct. Pair programming is an agile software development technique in which two developers work side-by-side: one programmer writes the code, the other reviews the code as it is entered. In this manner, the feedback loop is immediate and is the shortest of any other available options.

Explanation:

The scenario describes a hybrid project in which some of the elements are managed using a predictive/traditional project management approach (the schedule baseline, the Control Quality process, the dedicated QA department) while others are managed using agile (the product is developed over the course of several iterations).

Pair programming is an agile software development technique from eXtreme Programming (XP) in which two developers work side-by-side in tandem at the same workstation. While one programmer writes the code, the other reviews the code as it is entered. The two then switch roles frequently. With pair programming, the feedback loop is immediate. If a developer enters a coding error, their partner has the opportunity to catch the error where it can be fixed immediately. Thus, of the available responses, pair programming offers the feedback loop with the shortest interval.

References:

Agile Practice Guide – First Edition, Project Management Institute Inc, 2018, Page(s) 102

The Software Project Manager's Bridge to Agility, Michele Sliger, Stacia Broderick, 2008, XP

Did you get it right?

The PMP exam is not just for IT project managers, but pair programming is, of course, a coding technique. Project managers from non-IT industries may get this question wrong because they would not necessarily know what pair programming is.

Having said that, it's not guaranteed that project managers with an IT background will know what pair programming is either. If they took a basic agile class, or aren't yet certified at all, they may never have heard of pair programming, which is a technique from eXtreme Programming (XP).

And even if they have heard about pair programming, and understand that it reduces defects, increases quality and reduced the need for rework, it still takes a leap to deduce that this could also 'reduce the feedback loop'.

Typically, we think about the feedback loop as communication between the developers and the customers/stakeholders. But if you are reducing coding time by pair programming, that's not directly reducing the feedback loop; it's more of an indirect relationship.

The steps would be:

- Change over to pair programming
- Figure out who would be compatible as pair programmers
- Decide which development effort best lends itself to pair programming
- Implement pair programming
- Therefore, catch coding errors faster
- Therefore, reduce the feedback loop.

A much easier question about pair programming would be asking about its obvious benefits, like the reduction of errors, increased quality from catching errors before they go further downstream or how collaboration can lead to synergy between the two developers in each pair, further increasing quality.

There are three other responses where people often make mistakes: choosing shortening the iteration length, reducing the size of the user stories or revising the schedule baseline. Let's look at why those might have looked right at first glance and why you shouldn't have chosen them.

More on the iteration length
Even though shortening the iteration length is seldom done, it does make some sense that if you shortened the iteration length, that might help a little with reducing the feedback loop. It's not a completely bad answer, but it's not as good as the correct answer.

You might have chosen this option if you thought that it sounded 'cleaner'. In other words, if you concluded that with one simple action you could reduce the feedback loop.

More on user stories
By the same line of reasoning as for the iteration length response above, reducing the size of the user stories does sound like a way of simplifying the development challenges, which could also reduce the feedback loop.

And like the answer about iteration length, since this would be done in one shot, that might make it sound like a better choice. However, if you understand the purpose and benefits of pair programming, you can conclude that is the better answer.

More on the schedule baseline
This answer does not really sound like it would solve the problem. However,

because the question includes the Control Quality process name, which is clearly a term from the predictive approach, you might be tempted to select it because it's the only choice about predictive approaches.

A15 Question 15: Answer

The project manager has just completed gathering and documenting the requirements for a construction project in accordance with the scope management plan. Using decomposition along with other relevant tools and techniques, the project manager needs to create the scope baseline.

Based on this information, in what order will the following tasks need to be completed? (In your exam, on a question like this you would be asked to drag and drop the items from right to left. In this book, please arrange the answer choices in the correct order.)

Answer choices	Answers
Step one	
Step two	
Step three	
Step four	
Step five	
Step six	
(Not applicable)	

- Determine the planning packages of the WBS
- Create the project scope statement
- Finalize the WBS dictionary
- Identify control accounts for the WBS
- Document the work package cost estimates
- Develop the work packages for the WBS
- Gain approval for the scope baseline

Answers:

Answer choices	Answers (correct order)
Step one	**Create the project scope statement**
Step two	**Identify control accounts for the WBS**
Step three	**Determine the planning packages of the WBS**
Step four	**Develop the work packages for the WBS**
Step five	**Finalize the WBS dictionary**
Step six	**Gain approval for the scope baseline**
(Not applicable)	**Document the work package cost estimates**

Explanation:

The question implies that the Collect Requirements process has been completed, and now the project manager needs to create the scope baseline, which is an output of the Create WBS process. The scope baseline is the approved version of the scope statement, work breakdown structure (WBS), and its associated WBS dictionary. Therefore, the project manager will need to follow the logical steps necessary to create the scope statement, WBS, and WBS dictionary.

Once requirements have been gathered, the first step in creating the scope baseline will be to develop the project scope statement. The project scope statement is comprised of a description of the project scope, major deliverables, and exclusions. The project scope statement serves as an input to creating the WBS, and WBS dictionary; thus, the project scope statement must be created first.

The work breakdown structure (WBS) is a hierarchical decomposition of the total scope of work to be carried out by the project team to accomplish the project objectives and create the required deliverables. The creation of the WBS requires the scope to be decomposed into control accounts, planning packages, and work packages. The planning package is a WBS component below the control account level, and the work packages represent the lowest level. Thus, the WBS would be decomposed starting with the control accounts, then the planning packages, and finally the work packages.

The WBS dictionary is a document that provides a detailed deliverable, activity, and scheduling information about each component in the work breakdown structure. Since the WBS dictionary is dependent upon the information provided in the WBS, the WBS must be completed before the WBS dictionary can be finalized.

Finally, since the scope baseline is the approved version of the scope statement, work breakdown structure (WBS), and its associated WBS dictionary, the project manager will need to gain approval for the scope baseline as an element of the project management plan.

Note that the work package cost estimates are a component of the cost baseline rather than the scope baseline. Since the question only asked about the scope baseline, this answer choice can be excluded.

Reference:
A Guide to the Project Management Body of Knowledge, (*PMBOK® Guide*) – Sixth Edition, Project Management Institute Inc., 2017, Page(s) 154, 161-162

Did you get it right?

There isn't a strict rule that says that control accounts, planning packages and work packages have to be created in that order. In fact, some project managers build the WBS from the bottom up, and that's mentioned in the *PMBOK® Guide* as a legitimate option.

However, sometimes you have to deal with ambiguity in the questions. Even though these three artifacts don't exactly have to be created in the above order, they do have to end up in that order visually on the WBS. To arrive at that conclusion, you have to let go of the literal meaning of 'have to be created in that order', even though that's what the question says.

It wouldn't make sense to put them in a different order on a WBS, or on this test question.

In real life, some project managers no doubt create the WBS first and the other two later. Even if you are one of those project managers who does it that way, you should be able to reason-out the above order for the test question, based on how these three do end up in that order on the WBS.

By definition, the work package is the lowest level at the bottom, so work packages fall under control packages, and planning packages fall in the middle, as described in the *PMBOK® Guide* and other books.

Another reason why this is very tough is there are seven choices, and you need to choose six, and eliminate one (in just over a minute). That is a lot of work. If you make any mistake in the order, even if you choose all six correctly, and you get the question 100% wrong, having wasted probably at least two minutes, which could have been better spent answering two shorter or easier questions.

For time management on the exam, be on the lookout for questions that will take a long time to answer, and be ready to guess on a long one and mark it for later.

More on cost estimates
Another difficult thing about this question is that some diagrams in PMP prep books show the cost estimates in the work packages. If you've seen that, you may likely think that documenting the work package cost estimates is a correct response.

You have to recognize that cost estimates can be inside work packages, and know that cost estimates is incorrect because those are used for the performance baseline and not the scope baseline – even though cost estimates end up physically in the WBS, which is inside the scope baseline!

To understand that fairly subtle point, you have to know the difference between those two baselines, and many people have trouble differentiating the two.

Question 16: Answer

A16

A project manager has been assigned to a heavily-regulated drug development project that will use traditional waterfall phases combined with agile methodologies. Currently, the project manager is conducting a communication requirements analysis as part of the development of a communications management plan.

What is the best strategy to address the communication needs of this hybrid project?

A) Determine directions of influence of each project stakeholder and include the results in the communications management plan
B) Ensure that only the regulatory compliance elements of the project are included in the communications management plan
✓ **C) Develop the requirements list specific to the waterfall phases and use regulatory obligations as overarching requirements for all phases**
D) A communications management plan is not necessary when some of the project phases are executed using an agile approach.

All answers:

A) Determine directions of influence of each project stakeholder and include the results in the communications management plan
Incorrect. Directions of influence are an example of the data

representation technique that may be used as part of the Identify Stakeholders process. The results of this analysis are typically used for the development of the stakeholder register and stakeholder engagement plan, rather than the communications management plan.

B) Ensure that only the regulatory compliance elements of the project are included in the communications management plan
Incorrect. While addressing the regulatory compliance elements in the communications management plan is necessary for the drug development project that is heavily regulated, the plan should not be limited to only one specific aspect. The communications management plan should address all communication requirements collected during the Plan Communications Management process described in the scenario.

✓ C) **Develop the requirements list specific to the waterfall phases and use regulatory obligations as overarching requirements for all phases**
Correct. A detailed requirements list will be needed for the communications management plan as it applies to the waterfall aspects of the project. Compliance with regulatory obligations will be mandatory for the project regardless of the project management framework.

D) A communications management plan is not necessary when some of the project phases are executed using an agile approach.
Incorrect. A communications management plan may not always be necessary for a purely agile project. However, the question indicates that some phases of the project will utilize a waterfall model. A communications management plan is typically an important element for waterfall projects.

Explanation:
The scenario describes a hybrid project that is combining predictive and agile methodologies. Waterfall projects (or phases in this case) should have a fully-developed communications plan included as an element of the project management plan. Agile best practices advocate maximizing the amount of work not done; thus, plans and documentation are reduced to what is barely sufficient.

However, even though agile methodologies seek to minimize plans and documentation, regulatory requirements are an element of the project that must be complied with regardless of the project management framework. Therefore, even though some phases of the project will be managed using an agile framework, the project will need an overarching plan to ensure compliance with regulatory required communication.

References:
A Guide to the Project Management Body of Knowledge, (*PMBOK® Guide*) – Sixth Edition, Project Management Institute Inc., 2017, Page(s) 369-370

Agile Practice Guide – First Edition, Project Management Institute Inc, 2018, Page(s) 9

Did you get it right?

This question sets up a very challenging scenario: how best to create a Communication Management Plan under three competing constraints:

- The team is working on creating a predictive planning component (the Communication Management Plan)
- But in a Hybrid Environment
- And under "the heavily regulated drug development world" (the pharma industry).

A predictive planning component on a semi-agile project is somewhat of a contradiction, because some of the agile team-members would likely view it as an unnecessary, resource-wasting documentation exercise.

Adding to the challenge of the question are two more unknowns:

- Every hybrid environment is unique, with no clear 'rules' about how to handle the two competing halves of waterfall and agile, so there are no rules to guide you to the correct answer.
- When test takers see something very industry-specific, like the project taking place 'in the drug development world' it can be intimidating. They don't know the specifics of that world, and there is some fear that they will be expected to know something about the EEFs of the industry which, in this case, is famous for having strict, specific EEFs, rules, and protocols, and serious laws that guide projects and must be followed to avoid legal repercussions.

When given an industry-specific scenario, like drug-related/pharma in this question, focus on the key fact, which in this question is 'heavily-regulated.' Don't be distracted too much by the industry and remember that you can't be expected to know much about any one industry.

Look for what the question is expecting you to know and use that to get to the answer.

This challenge is made even harder by the fact the four choices are unusually long. Let's look at the incorrect choices to see why you might have chosen then.

A) Determine directions of influence of each project stakeholder and include the results in the communications management plan

This sounds good, and there's nothing incorrect about the statement, but this is more for Stakeholder Management than Communications Management. However, Stakeholder Management and Communications Management go hand-in-hand and are heavily-related, so you have to try to remember if the relevant stakeholder tools and outputs could be valid inputs here.

And forgetting for a moment about the *PMBOK® Guide*, it's possible that the project manager would take the directions of influence into account when communicating with the stakeholders, and therefore might feel it should go into the Communications Plan.

It is worth spending some extra time studying the differences between the closely-related topics of communication and stakeholder management so that you have a clear grasp of which uses which inputs and tools.

B) Ensure that only the regulatory compliance elements of the project are included in the communications management plan
The key word about this choice is 'only'. If you miss the word, you may have incorrectly opted for this answer.

If you read the question carefully, it's easy to eliminate this choice.

☑ **C) Develop requirements list specific to the waterfall phases and use regulatory obligations as overarching requirements for all phases**
This is the correct answer – however, there are two tricky things about the wording that could have led you to discount the choice.

First, using the term 'requirements list' may be confusing for some test takers because that sounds a lot like the 'requirements document' from the Collect Requirements process in the Scope Management knowledge area.

That could make the test taker wonder if this is the wrong answer because it's stepping outside the Communications Management knowledge area where the question is based.

Second, it's confusing that this choice uses the word 'phases' twice, and in two different ways. It's not exactly clear what is meant by 'waterfall phases' or 'all phases'.

Even more confusing is the fact that this choice uses them in slightly different language, and order, from the way the question also uses the word 'phases' twice. In the question, 'phases' refers to traditional agile and waterfall phases.

The *PMBOK® Guide* has a very specific meaning for phases. The term is used to mean that on a very large project, you might break it up into, for instance, three phases, with each treated like a project in that the full set of domain knowledge is applied to each.

D) A communications management plan is not necessary when some of the project phases are executed using an agile approach.
This choice is pretty obviously incorrect, because the whole point of the scenario is about creating the Communications Management Plan.

However, some test takers who have a strong agile background or mindset might consider selecting this choice because agile values of working software over comprehensive documentation as stated in the Manifesto.

This choice is the more extreme case of an agilist rejecting documentation altogether, which is not correct.

This question is another example of where your internalized assumptions and preferences may lead you to choose the wrong answer. Or we could say: agilists: Check your anti-waterfall attitude at the door (at least while taking the PMP exam!).

If only for the sake of passing your PMP exam, take a moment to self-reflect on whether you have an anti-waterfall bias, and if you feel that you do, make a conscious effort to not let that push you to wrong answers on your test.

Question 17: Answer

A traditionally managed project is using Scrum to develop the project deliverables. The agile release plan calls for the recently completed MVP to be deployed into production. However, the quality assurance (QA) department rejects the MVP, stating that the department's policies and procedures do not address the implementation of interim deliverables.

After recording the issue on the impediment board, what should the project manager do next?

A) Submit a change request to update the quality control measurements
☑ **B) Request the project sponsor's help with obtaining the necessary approvals**
C) Ignore the QA department's opinion and release the MVP as scheduled
D) Ask the project team to deliver a feature-complete product before deployment

All answers:

A) Submit a change request to update the quality control measurements
Incorrect. Quality control measurements are the documented results of the activities carried out as part of the Control Quality process. First, quality control measurements are considered a project document and, as such, do not require a change request to be updated. Second, the issue described in the scenario lies with the policies and procedures of the QA department rather than the way the Control Quality activities are carried out.

☑ **B) Request the project sponsor's help with obtaining the necessary approvals**
Correct. The project manager should make every effort to remove the organizational impediment to meet the release plan and ensure that the intended benefits of the MVP are realized as soon as possible.

C) Ignore the QA department's opinion and release the MVP as scheduled
Incorrect. With some exceptions, answer choices that include the word "ignore" typically represent incorrect responses. Ignoring the opinion of the QA department is unlikely to be the best course of action for a project manager.

D) Ask the project team to deliver a feature-complete product before deployment
Incorrect. Since the MVP represents value to the organization, the project manager should seek to overcome the organizational impediment and get the MVP deployed as soon as possible. Only after all reasonable efforts fail to get the MVP delivered into production should the team wait until the software is feature-complete for deployment.

Explanation:

The scenario describes a hybrid project, which incorporates elements of predictive and agile frameworks. In the scenario, the team has created a minimal viable product (MVP) that is ready for release. One of the objectives of agile methodologies is to deliver value incrementally so that project benefits can be realized as soon as possible rather than waiting until the end of the project.

The fact that the quality assurance department lacks policies and procedures for interim deliverables represents an organizational impediment. One of the responsibilities of the project manager as a servant leader is to address and remove impediments, obstacles, and blockers for the team so that the team can deliver the most value to the organization.

In this case, the project manager should collaborate with the quality assurance department to revise the policies and procedures to permit the delivery of the MVP. If those efforts fail, then the next logical step would be to escalate the issue to the project sponsor. Since working directly with the quality assurance department to resolve the issue was not offered as an answer choice, the best answer, of the choices provided, is to escalate the issue to the project sponsor to remove the organizational impediment.

Note, the term 'impediment board' is used in the Agile Practice Guide as specified in the reference.

References:
A Guide to the Project Management Body of Knowledge, (*PMBOK® Guide*) – Sixth Edition, Project Management Institute Inc., 2017, Page(s) 216

Agile Practice Guide – First Edition, Project Management Institute Inc, 2018, Page(s) 35, 59

Project Management Professional (PMP)® Examination Content Outline, Project Management Institute Inc., June 2019, Domain I, Task 7

Did you get it right?

Here are some reasons why a test taker might not get this question right.

They do not have a good understanding of the agile mindset. Many PMP candidates come from a largely waterfall background. Even though the environment described in this scenario suggests hybrid, you have to lean heavily to the agile side to get this one.

They may not understand the concept of an MVP. If they believe it is just an early version that isn't really anything much, it might seem likely that the Quality Assurance (QA) department doesn't want the MVP going into production.

They fail to read the question properly. The question is asking "What should the project manager do next?" If the project manager ignores the QA Department and just releases the MVP, that could be grounds for dismissal. They do want to release the MVP, but it's important to use the proper channels. That is exactly where the product owner comes in, to liaise between the project manager and the stakeholders, including the QA team in this example.

There is no reason to assume that the product owner is not on board with putting in the MVP, given that they would have been heavily involved in the creation of the product backlog and in on many of the ceremonies of this project.

Let's look at the other two other areas where a close look at the topic can help you make the right choice.

More on MVPs

The project is being done in scrum sprints, where the whole point is delivering in increments. Given that, it makes no sense to reject the MVP on the grounds that it's not the full-product yet.

Test takers who come from a mainly waterfall background may lean toward choice D, thinking that if the QA department says they are not in compliance with current company requirements, they had better go back and deliver the full product with all features. That is wrong, because it was decided to run the product with Scrum, and an MVP is a perfect example of good early incremental delivery.

Many Agilists like releasing an MVP early, and then adding more to it later to make it stronger, after the customer has gotten early value from the MVP.

That was the agreement for Scrum being selected for this project, to create deliverables in increments, and more specifically, to create an MVP.

So caving in to the QA department is not appropriate at all here – it's going against the entire plan for this project. Maybe it might make sense in a waterfall environment sometimes to respond to the QA team in that way, but here it's very wrong.

In a hybrid environment, you would lean toward the rules of the methodology the team is primarily working in. If you're working in Scrum, as the question states, it would be wrong to make a decision that undercuts the scrum mindset in a big way.

More on measurements

It would not be appropriate to submit a change request for measurements since measurements are live data, and not something to be changed.

It would not be a bad idea to submit a change request about the QA departments' policies and procedures, but that is not an available choice for this question.

The more appropriate, more decisive, more effective, and faster way to get the MVP approved and moved into production is to use the support of the product owner. Again, this relies on the test taker having an understanding of the agile mindset and scrum methodology.

A18 Question 18: Answer

You have joined a project in which requirements are elaborated at several intervals during delivery, and the delivery is divided into subsets of the overall product. Change is incorporated at periodic intervals, and risk and cost are controlled by progressively elaborating the plans with new information. Key stakeholders are regularly involved.

What development approach is used on your project?

   A) Agile
   B) Predictive
✓ **C) Hybrid**
   D) Periodic

All answers:

   A) Agile
       Incorrect. On agile projects, requirements are elaborated frequently during delivery; delivery occurs frequently with customer-valued subsets of the overall product; change is incorporated in real-time during delivery; risk and cost are controlled as requirements and constraints emerge; and, key stakeholders are continuously involved.

   B) Predictive
       Incorrect. On predictive projects, requirements are defined up-front before development begins; a single final product is delivered at the end of the project; change is constrained as much as possible; risk and cost are controlled by detailed planning; and, key stakeholders are involved at specific milestones.

✓ **C) Hybrid**
       Correct. On hybrid projects, requirements are elaborated at several intervals; delivery is divided into subsets of the overall product; change is incorporated at periodic intervals; risk and cost are controlled by progressively elaborating the plans with new information; and, key stakeholders are regularly involved. This is the exact match with the scenario described, making this choice the best answer to the question asked.

   D) Periodic
       Incorrect. 'Periodic' is not a development approach specified in the reference provided. It's a term that was made-up for this question.

Explanation:

Development approach is a component of the project management plan that describes, as the name implies, the approach selected for the development of the product, service, or result delivered by the project. Predictive, iterative, agile, or hybrid are examples of the development approach. The main differences between the various development approaches lie in the way requirements are defined and managed, project deliverables are produced, change is handled, risk and cost are controlled, and stakeholders are involved. The different development approaches can be visually displayed on what is called, the continuum of project life cycles.

A predictive development approach is at one extreme of the continuum, while the agile approach is at the other end, with hybrid models being anywhere in between. The scenario describes a project in which requirements are elaborated at several intervals during delivery; the delivery is divided into subsets of the overall product; change is incorporated at periodic intervals; risk and cost are controlled by progressively elaborating the plans with new information; and, key stakeholders are regularly involved. These practices combine elements of both predictive and agile life cycles, making the whole development approach hybrid.

Note, the development approach is sometimes called the development life cycle.

Reference:
A Guide to the Project Management Body of Knowledge, (*PMBOK® Guide*) – Sixth Edition, Project Management Institute Inc., 2017, Page(s) 666, 88

Did you get it right?
This is a very tough question because the scenario walks a fine line between agile and hybrid.

There is a fair degree of ambiguity in the scenario. There is more evidence of agile than predictive approaches. They might choose the agile answer because they can definitely see that, but they aren't sure if predictive if making an appearance.

Assuming we can quickly rule out periodic as a made-up term that is obviously wrong, let's look at the other choices.

Agile
We can be pretty sure the project in the scenario is using agile methods from this phrase in the question: "the delivery is divided into subsets of the overall project."

This suggests incremental delivery which is a hallmark of agile (notably Scrum, but not limited to Scrum).

This presents a strong argument for choosing this option.

Predictive
The same phrase: "the delivery is divided into subsets of the overall project" largely tells us that the product is not being managed in a predictive way. A

classic predictive approach delivers one final deliverable at the end of the project, and not subsets along the way.

That helps us rule out this option. However, there is one exception to consider, and that is when a predictive project is delivered in phases which might give deliverables in sub-sets.

Hybrid

There is enough in the question to suggest a somewhat predictive environment, combined with the agile that is also present in the project, and that gives us a hybrid environment as the correct choice.

There is deliberately some ambiguity in the scenario between what is agile and what is predictive, making this a challenging question for the following reasons.

- Requirements are elaborated at several intervals during delivery. At first read, 'several intervals' sounds like it could mean scrum sprints. However, the word 'several' pushes the scenario away from Scrum and more towards predictive approaches. For example, a scrum project with 15 sprints would require 15 sprint backlog planning selections, and 15 would not be described as several intervals.
- The question says that change is incorporated at periodic intervals, and risk and cost are controlled by progressively elaborating the plans with new information. 'Periodic intervals' might suggest Scrum (periodic could mean, for instance, every two weeks), but at the core of the agile change-friendly mindset, is the fact that change is handled on an as-needed basis. Change at scheduled intervals is how change is often handled in Predictive.
- Key stakeholders are regularly involved. This sounds at first like Scrum, because the customer is represented in the scrum retros and scrum demos. However, on close scrutiny, it's not necessarily Scrum, because it doesn't pinpoint one key stakeholder who is present at all the standups each day in Scrum, as well as at all the major scrum ceremonies. Because it's plural (stakeholders) that makes it sound less like the product owner filling the role. On many predictive projects, it's often true that key stakeholders are regularly involved, so there is some ambiguity.
- Delivery is divided into subsets of the overall product. Even though this strongly suggests agile, especially sprints, it could be a predictive project that is broken up into phases, for example.
- Finally, we know from the scenario that risk and cost are controlled by progressively elaborating the plans with new information. This sounds mainly like a predictive situation. However, there is some ambiguity here

as well. If someone is thinking about Scrum and looks at this sentence, they could be thinking that the way the sprint backlog gets re-examined, changed, and finalized before each sprint, that could be considered "progressively elaborating the plans with new information".

A19 Question 19: Answer

To promote continuous improvement, your organization uses a methodology that involves defining the objectives and scope of the project, measuring to obtain data, analyzing the collected data to find the root causes, improving by developing a solution, and controlling by evaluating the implemented solution.

What quality improvement method is your organization using?

A) Total quality management (TQM)
✓ **B) Six Sigma**
C) Quality function deployment (QFD)
D) Deming's PDCA cycle

All answers:

A) Total quality management (TQM)
Incorrect. TQM describes a management approach to long-term success through customer satisfaction. In a TQM effort, all members of an organization participate in improving processes, products, services, and the culture in which they work. While TQM is concerned with quality, the scenario describes the five phases of Six Sigma, define, measure, analyze, improve, and control and, therefore, TQM is not the correct choice.

✓ **B) Six Sigma**
Correct. Define, measure, analyze, improve, and control are the steps described in the scenario for the methodology used by your organization. These are the five phases of the Six Sigma quality improvement method.

C) Quality function deployment (QFD)
Incorrect. QFD is a structured method that uses seven management and planning tools, such as affinity diagrams, relations diagrams, tree diagrams, and so on, to identify and prioritize customers' expectations quickly and effectively. The scenario describes the five phases of Six Sigma, define, measure, analyze, improve, and control, not the tools of QFD.

D) Deming's PDCA cycle
Incorrect. Deming's PDCA cycle is a four-step quality cycle consisting of

plan, do, check, and act. The scenario describes the five phases of Six Sigma, define, measure, analyze, improve, and control.

Explanation:

The Six Sigma method of quality improvement focuses on increasing the effectiveness and efficiencies of projects and eliminating defects and waste. The Six Sigma method is more comprehensive than prior process improvement initiatives such as Total Quality Management (TQM) and Continuous Quality Improvement (CQI).

The scenario describes the steps in the methodology currently in place in your organization. Those steps are the phases of Six Sigma:

- Define: The objectives and scope of the project are defined. Relevant information about the process and customer are collected.
- Measure: Data on the current situation and process metrics are collected.
- Analyze: Collected data are analyzed to find the root cause(s) of the problem.
- Improve: Solution(s) to the problem are developed and implemented.
- Control: The implemented solution(s) are evaluated, and mechanisms are implemented to hold the gains, which may include standardization.

Therefore, based on the description of these steps, the quality improvement method your organization uses is Six Sigma.

The topic of this question is only briefly mentioned in the *PMBOK® Guide*. However, the Project Management Professional (PMP)® Examination Content Outline (ECO) indicates that while there are some commonalities between the *PMBOK® Guide* and the ECO, the exam is not bound by the *PMBOK® Guide*.

The list of enablers specified in the tasks of the ECO domains is not exhaustive either. The ECO assumes that prospective PMP aspirants are familiar with other sources of information/preparation, including but not limited to PMI Code of Ethics and Professional Conduct, PMI's Practice Standards (e.g. Scheduling, Earned Value Management, etc.), organizational behavior theories such as Tuckman's Ladder, Theory X and Theory Y, Maslow's hierarchy of needs, commonly frowned upon project management practices, such as gold plating, and others.

We intentionally have these questions in our simulator so that you would be better prepared for the real exam. PMP aspirants are encouraged to explore additional sources of information and/or to be familiar with them from their project management experience.

References:

A Guide to the Project Management Body of Knowledge, (*PMBOK® Guide*) – Sixth Edition, Project Management Institute Inc., 2017, Page(s) 296, 275

https://www.pmi.org/learning/library/six-sigma-method-applications-pm-8515

Did you get it right?

Here are some reasons why test takers get this question wrong.

- They are not familiar with the five phases of Six Sigma, which are not mentioned in the *PMBOK® Guide* (although Six Sigma itself is mentioned briefly). Most PMP prep books only talk about Six Sigma as a way of describing very high quality: 99.99966% – the 'Five Nines'.
- They are not familiar with how Six Sigma is used for calculating control limits on control charts (as three Sigma above and three Sigma below the Mean).
- They are confused by the mention of continuous improvement. This is commonly referred to as Kaizen which is commonly attributed to Deming. Choice D mentions Deming specifically, so that might look like the right option – even though PDCA is four steps and Six Sigma has five phases, that might send some test takers down the wrong path.

Another area of difficulty with this question is that since many students will associate Six Sigma with very high quality, 99.99966% quality (the Five Nines) or calculating the mean on Control Charts, that might lead them to reject Six Sigma as the answer because the answer choice doesn't reflect what they know about Six Sigma, and then incorrectly guess either A (TQM) or C (QFD).

It will be the rare student who gets this question right! But that's what makes the question valuable for your PMP exam prep. Remember to study from other sources, and be aware that the *PMBOK® Guide* and Agile Practice Guide alone are not enough.

Question 20: Answer

Project stakeholders meet to discuss the threat of a severe staff shortage due to a potential union workers' strike that might take place during project execution. With various response strategies on the table, the stakeholders want to make a decision as to how to address the issue should the threat occur.

What response strategy will the stakeholders be using while deciding to implement one of the following decisions? (In your exam, on a question like this you would be asked to drag and drop the items from right to left. In this book, please arrange the answer choices in the correct order.)

Answer choices	Answers
Cancel the project	
Outsource staffing	
Automate processes	
Hire reserve workers	
Delegate to management	

- Escalate
- Avoid
- Mitigate
- Transfer
- Accept

Answers:

Answer choices	Answers (correct order)
Cancel the project	**Avoid**
Outsource staffing	**Transfer**
Automate processes	**Mitigate**
Hire reserve workers	**Accept**
Delegate to management	**Escalate**

Explanation:

Risk avoidance is when the project team acts to eliminate the threat or protect the project from its impact. The avoid strategy, including project cancellation, may be adopted when the level of overall project risk is significantly negative.

Transferring the risk involves shifting ownership of a threat to a third party to manage the risk and bear the impact if it occurs. Examples of risk transferring include the use of insurance, warranties, guarantees, etc. These actions typically involve payment of a risk premium to the party taking on the threat.

In risk mitigation, the action is taken to reduce the probability and/or impact of a risk. Automating processes aims to do just that (assuming some project tasks can be done automatically rather than manually).

When a risk is actively accepted, its existence is acknowledged, but no immediate proactive action is taken; instead, a reserve is put in place. Hiring reserve workers are an example of risk acceptance.

Lastly, when escalating risk to management, a project team acknowledges that decision-making related to the risk is out of the project team's control and beyond their level of authority.

Reference:
A Guide to the Project Management Body of Knowledge, (*PMBOK® Guide*) – Sixth Edition, Project Management Institute Inc., 2017, Page(s) 442-443

Did you get it right?

Three of the five choices are very easy to match: Avoid, Transfer and Escalate.

However, the other two, as presented in this question are harder.

This is largely because Accept has two flavors in risk management, one well-known and one not well-known. They are:

- Passive Acceptance (very well-known and the way it's almost always used)
- Active Acceptance (not well-known)

Most questions and books assume passive acceptance, and that is the true in the common usage of English too, outside the project management world.

For example, someone might ask:

"Are you just going to accept the risk of your car being stolen, or are you going to do something about it?"

a) make sure to lock your car
b) park in a well-lit area
c) install a steering wheel lock
d) buy insurance.

Most project managers would think the above four choices were mitigation responses, not acceptance of the risk, because they are proactive actions to reduce the probability of having your car stolen. However, it could be argued that they are 'active acceptance' in that even doing all four brings no absolute guarantee of not having your car stolen.

If the match for Accept was 'take no action at this time' that would look much more like acceptance the way most people think of the word. No one would match Mitigate with 'take no action at this time'.

Because the match for Accept is not very obvious, that adds ambiguity choosing the match for Automate processes.

Automating processes is pretty clearly mitigating both the likelihood and the impact of a worker strike.

However, many project managers might look at hiring reserve workers as a form of mitigation as well, in both senses of the meaning of 'mitigate', which are:

- Probability: By hiring reserve workers, you are reducing the likelihood of a strike, because with a lot more workers, it might be tougher for the union to their members to vote for a strike, as they will see there are replacements on-site ready and willing to take their jobs and pay checks.
- Impact: By hiring reserve workers, even if there is a strike, the impact will be lessened, because there will definitely be more workers there to pick up the slack.

Of the five strategies for negative risk (threats), be very aware that in project management and on the PMP test, both 'mitigate' and 'accept' have two meanings, per the *PMBOK® Guide*.

Question 21: Answer

You are in charge of a large project to install 5G internet hubs across your city. Although most of the project variables are clear and can be managed using the waterfall approach, technical aspects are not fully defined and will be elaborated as the project progresses. The sponsor requests that project information will be communicated more frequently and quickly.

To address the sponsor's request, you will use all of the following, except:

A) Holding frequent team checkpoints
B) Conducting regular stakeholder reviews
C) Implementing information radiators
✓ **D) Communicating project status weekly**

All answers:

A) Holding frequent team checkpoints
Incorrect. Frequent team checkpoints refer to agile practices such as daily standups, iteration reviews, retrospectives, etc. While it is unclear from the scenario if the team can or need to meet daily and whether the deliverables are built using iterations, frequent team checkpoints would address the sponsor request for more frequent and quick communication.

B) Conducting regular stakeholder reviews
Incorrect. Unlike traditional projects where stakeholders are involved

in key milestones and gates, agile projects benefit from regular stakeholder reviews and continuous engagement. Conducting regular stakeholder reviews would support the sponsor's request to have more frequent and quick communications on the project.

C) Implementing information radiators
Incorrect. Information radiators are visible physical or digital displays that provide information to the rest of the organization enabling up-to-the-minute knowledge sharing. These displays help communicate progress, share issues, drive continuous improvement, and manage stakeholder expectations.

☑ **D) Communicating project status weekly**
Correct. It is unclear if weekly cadence would be considered by the sponsor to be frequent and quick enough. However, this option describes the practice that would 'least' likely support the need expressed by the sponsor to communicate project information more frequently and quickly, making this choice the best answer to the question asked.

Explanation:
The scenario describes a project with mainly stable and known upfront elements, allowing the project manager to apply a waterfall project management approach. Technical aspects of the project, on the other hand, are not yet fully defined and will be elaborated as the project progresses. This implies some agile practices will be required to manage these unclear aspects, resulting in an overall hybrid project management approach. Project environments subject to various elements of ambiguity and change have an inherent need to communicate evolving and emerging details more frequently and quickly. In such environments, project managers should encourage frequent team checkpoints, the use of information radiators, and holding regular stakeholder reviews.

While it is unclear whether sending the project report on a weekly basis considered by the sponsor to be frequent enough, the incorrect answer choices describe agile communication practices that would support the need for frequent and quick communication of project information. Sending the project report on a weekly basis is the only choice that stands out as non-agile and, therefore, will likely be an exception to your selection of tools and techniques, making this choice the best answer to the question asked.

Reference:
A Guide to the Project Management Body of Knowledge, (*PMBOK® Guide*) – Sixth Edition, Project Management Institute Inc., 2017, Page(s) 365

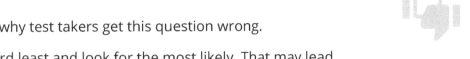

Did you get it right?

Here are some reasons why test takers get this question wrong.

- They miss the word least and look for the most likely. That may lead them to choose the option about holding frequent team checkpoints, which is clearly a good thing to do.
- They overlook the word least and choose the option about information radiators, which is the best way to communicate on many projects, and it's also clearly an agile way, which the question is looking for.
- They get confused between choices B and D as they both sound like they could be either correct or incorrect, even after several readings!
- They don't realize that stakeholder reviews are a way of increasing communications. In reality, conducting regular stakeholder reviews is a good way to increase communications, but this is an indirect way of saying it. Stakeholder reviews are good, and they result in good communications, but stakeholder reviews don't exactly sound like communication. They are often not considered communication in the same way that an information radiator clearly is.

The choice about communicating project status weekly is very much about communication, and it sounds positive. However, once a week meetings are very much a waterfall approach.

They are not considered timely compared to daily standup meetings, which have largely replaced them in many environments – and not only agile environments. It might sound like a good choice, but in the context of the scenario it's the least good option which makes it the right answer for this question.

Question 22: Answer

A22

As product increments are developed and then deployed at customer premises, the customer initiates new requirements, submits changes, and reports defects. The requirements, changes, and defects are reviewed by the CCB comprised of the project manager, product owner, and team, and prioritized for the upcoming iterations. The scope baseline is updated accordingly.

How should the work on the new requirements, changes, and defects be carried out?

- A) As specified in the requirements traceability matrix
- B) According to the organizational process assets
- ✓ **C) Using a single-list-of-work-and-changes approach**
- D) By implementing enterprise environmental factors

All answers:

A) As specified in the requirements traceability matrix
Incorrect. The requirements traceability matrix is a project document in the form of a grid that links product requirements from their origin to the deliverables that satisfy them. This document does not have any guidelines as to how work to implement requirements, changes, and defect repairs should be carried out on a project.

B) According to the organizational process assets
Incorrect. Organizational process assets (OPAs) are the processes, policies, and procedures specific to and used by the performing organization. While the OPAs may contain guidelines on how work should be carried out in the organization in general, each project has its own specific instructions, typically outlined in the project management plan.

☑ C) **Using a single-list-of-work-and-changes approach**
Correct. This term, 'single-list-of-work-and-changes' refers to the product backlog, which is, as its name implies, a list of items such as requirements, changes, and defect repairs that should be completed during the project. The list is prioritized, and the items are pulled out by the project team from the top of the backlog.

D) By implementing enterprise environmental factors
Incorrect. Enterprise environmental factors (EEFs) are conditions, not under the control of the project team, that influence, constrain, or direct the project. EEFs do not provide instructions as to how work should be carried out in projects and are not something that can be 'implemented'.

Explanation:
Similar to some other questions, this question describes a seemingly unusual project management approach in which elements of traditional methods (CCB, scope baseline) intertwine with agile practices (product increments, iterations). Such a combination of methods from different project management methodologies results in a hybrid project management approach.

In the scenario, the product is developed in iterations, which typically (although not always) means the work items are organized as a backlog. The backlog is a list of work items prioritized by the product owner in consultation with the team and relevant stakeholders. New features/requirements, changes to existing features, and defect repairs for already developed product increments are considered work items. Therefore, it makes sense for the work to be carried out using a single-list-of-work-and-changes approach.

Reference:
A Guide to the Project Management Body of Knowledge, (*PMBOK® Guide*) – Sixth Edition,
Project Management Institute Inc., 2017, Page(s) 671

Did you get it right?

This is a tricky question because the correct term appears only once, in the appendix (check the reference above for it).

However, even if you had never heard the term before, you would probably be able to work out the correct answer because 'single-list-of-work-and-changes' approach does sound like it fits the scenario.

Here's why some test takers might have got this one wrong:

- They chose the requirements traceability matrix because the scenario sounds like a hybrid environment, where maybe using the matrix as the place where the requirements are kept (and if they are constantly updated accurately) might be a way to make this project succeed.
- They might believe 'single-list-of-work-and-changes' is a made-up term, and because they've heard of the requirements traceability matrix, they opted for that one.

Hopefully, you realized that OPAs and EEFs don't sound like the right answer at all.

The lesson here is that if you see a term you don't know, don't discount it automatically as being incorrect. Evaluate it to see if it sounds valid and could be a correct choice. Some of the terms can be obscure, but also, self-defining, meaning they mean what they sound like it means from the name.

Question 23: Answer

A large multi-year manufacturing project relies on traditional and agile methods to manage the vast project complexities and external dependencies. Due to those external dependencies, there are many challenges that cannot be addressed or budgeted for in the two-week iteration cycle.

How should the team address the longer-term budget challenges?

- ✓ **A) Facilitate a quarterly review of the budget and explore potential future budget challenges**
- B) Slowly inject more budgetary constraints and track the budget challenges that these constraints cause
- C) Steadily burn down the budget with every iteration and mitigate budget challenges
- D) Re-evaluate the budget after every iteration and add identified budget challenges to the risk register

All answers:

✓ **A) Facilitate a quarterly review of the budget and explore potential future budget challenges**

Correct. The blend of various project management methodologies requires the project team to leverage long term strategies of meeting quarterly to examine and address the budget requirements of the project. The shorter two-week cycles are not sufficient in addressing larger, more complex, budgetary challenges and project interdependencies.

B) Slowly inject more budgetary constraints and track the budget challenges that these constraints cause

Incorrect. The issue with the budget in this hybrid project is not the lack of constraints. As such, there is little advantage of injecting more constraints to the budget as the project progresses. Tracking budgetary challenges is a good practice, but not within the constraining measures.

C) Steadily burn down the budget with every iteration and mitigate budget challenges

Incorrect. The project budget does not get used equally and consumed over the project life cycle. The rate of how the budget is used is typically an S-curve in traditional projects. In a hybrid project, the rate differs. Basing the consumption of the budget on a steady per-iteration rate is most likely not feasible unless the expenditures are consistent and predictable.

D) Re-evaluate the budget after every iteration and add identified budget challenges to the risk register

Incorrect. It is true that with the portion of the project managed traditionally, any raised and identified budget risks should be entered into a risk register. However, taking this approach with the portion of the project that operates on a two-week iteration cycle would not be effective. Adding budget reviews after each cycle is considered overkill/counter-productive by many agile practitioners who would likely view this as not being aligned with the Agile Manifesto that values people and interactions over processes and tools.

Explanation:
A multi-year manufacturing hybrid project with two-week iteration cycles, such as the one described in the scenario, balances the shorter-term needs in an agile manner and the longer-term needs in a traditional plan-driven manner. Nonetheless, there are budgetary challenges that every project, regardless of the project management approach selected, must address. The larger the

scope and the greater the length of a project, the more interdependencies and budget challenges the project may encounter throughout its life cycle.

While, according to the scenario, the product of the project will be developed in two-week iterations, the question is asking about addressing the 'longer-term' budget challenges. Therefore, for this hybrid multi-year project, facilitating quarterly reviews of the budget would make the most sense in analyzing the current state as well as exploring and forecasting potential future budget challenges.

Reference:
A Guide to the Project Management Body of Knowledge, (*PMBOK® Guide*) – Sixth Edition, Project Management Institute Inc., 2017, Page(s) 254-256

Did you get it right?

This question tests your understanding of a hybrid project environment. The scenario must be analyzed well to get the answer. Choosing the right answer relies on understanding budgets in the real world, in light of both sprints and waterfall ways of working.

Hybrid can make for unique challenges on projects (and on test questions) because different approaches may apply to different parts of the project but there could be questions with analogous challenges such as about quality or scope etc.

It's not enough to think of hybrid as just a combination of waterfall and agile, but rather aim to understand the specifics of the particular hybrid environment on the question, and how that combination comes into play.

Question 24: Answer

A research project is characterized by high variability and uncertainty. The project scope is only known at a high level, so the WBS will have to be progressively elaborated throughout the project's life cycle. As the project manager estimates the team resources and various roles required for the project, she realizes that estimation is going to be a challenging task.

What is the best course of action for the project manager?

A) Adopt three-point estimating as a technique to determine the number of team members required for each role

B) Identify specific individuals to assign the roles of an agile coach, product owner, and cross-functional team members

✓ **C) Use analogous estimating to estimate the team resource requirements and include in the resource requirements document**

D) Estimate team resources at the activity level and then aggregate to develop estimates for work packages, control accounts, and summary project levels

All answers:

A) Adopt three-point estimating as a technique to determine the number of team members required for each role
Incorrect. Three-point estimating is among the tools and techniques that may be used to develop cost or duration estimates. However, three-point estimating is not likely to be used to determine team resource requirements and would not be particularly helpful in determining the specific roles that need to be filled.

B) Identify specific individuals to assign the roles of an agile coach, product owner, and cross-functional team members
Incorrect. Adopting a hybrid approach to include agile roles might be a good strategy for a project where the project scope cannot be decomposed during initial project planning. However, the question implies that the project manager is carrying out the Estimate Activity Resources process as part of project planning. Specific individuals would not be identified until the beginning of the execution stage as part of the Acquire Resources process.

☑ **C) Use analogous estimating to estimate the team resource requirements and include in the resource requirements document**
Correct. Using analogous estimating is an appropriate strategy to estimate team resources when a project manager can only identify the top levels of the WBS. While defining the various roles required for the project may be challenging at this point, of the choices provided, analogous estimating is the best answer to the question asked.

D) Estimate team resources at the activity level and then aggregate to develop estimates for work packages, control accounts, and summary project levels
Incorrect. This answer choice describes bottom-up estimating. Bottom-up estimating is a technique that can be used to estimate team resource requirements. However, bottom-up estimating requires a fully-decomposed work breakdown structure (WBS) and activity list, and the question stipulates that the project scope is only known at a high-level and the WBS will need to be progressively elaborated. Thus, using bottom-up estimating is not a viable strategy in this case.

Explanation:

The scenario implies that the project manager is carrying out the Estimate Activity Resources process as part of initial project planning and that only the top levels of the work breakdown structure (WBS) can be determined at this point. Thus, the project will need to use rolling wave planning or, more than likely, incorporate agile practices since projects with high variability and uncertainly benefit from an agile approach. Since the WBS cannot be fully decomposed at this point, analogous estimating is an appropriate strategy to estimate the team resource requirements.

Analogous estimating is a technique that uses information regarding resources from past similar projects as a basis for estimating the current project. The information can then be captured in the resource requirements document, which is an output of the Estimate Activity Resources process. It should be noted that the scenario does not explicitly state whether or not previous similar projects exist, but using analogous estimating is the only viable answer choice from among the alternatives provided.

References:

A Guide to the Project Management Body of Knowledge, (*PMBOK® Guide*) – Sixth Edition, Project Management Institute Inc., 2017, Page(s) 311, 325

Agile Practice Guide – First Edition, Project Management Institute Inc, 2018, Page(s) 7, 13

Effective Project Management: Traditional, Agile, Extreme, hybrid – 8th Edition, Robert K. Wysocki, 2019, Estimating Resource Requirements

Did you get it right?

Some test takers jump to the answer about agile roles, because that's the response that is not like the others. However, it's wrong! Some test takers use this approach to help them select the answer: they look for the one that does not look like the others. But just because it's not like the others does not make it the correct choice.

This is not a rule – perhaps it worked for questions on other exam papers in your past, but selecting the 'odd one out' will not help you on the PMP exam.

There are two very difficult challenges to this question.

First, both of the first two phrases in the question immediately and strongly suggest agile. In fact, those are the exact ways that are often used to differentiate which projects should be done as agile, versus which should be done as waterfall. That might lead you to start thinking about estimating in agile, and techniques like planning poker, Fibonacci, tee-shirt sizes, etc. However, three of the four answer choices are about predictive estimating techniques.

That might lead you to choose the agile answer, choice B, even though, that's really not a very good answer at all for solving the problem presented in the scenario.

Second, you have to know the types of estimating and then go beyond that to apply each type to estimating human resources.

Let's look at why the estimating techniques are particularly challenging in the context of this question.

More on estimating
This question is made difficult by the fact some of the estimating techniques are named and others are not.

Three-point estimating is specifically mentioned in choice A. Analogous estimating is specifically mentioned in choice C.

Bottom-up estimating is not specifically mentioned in choice D and is only suggested by the wording. That means you have to take two actions to evaluate choice D:

- Figure out that that this choice refers to bottom-up,
- And then decide whether bottom-up is the best answer here.

There's something else that makes choice D more difficult as well: it combines two kinds of bottom-up estimating.

Bottom-up estimating usually means estimating the individual low-level work packages and rolling them up. But choice D throws in a lot of elements that can go into bottom-up that are not work packages, like activities, control accounts and summary project levels.

It then brings in the term 'aggregate', all without using the term bottom-up estimating. You've got to evaluate all the terms, then identify the choice as bottom-up, and only then decide if that's the best kind of estimating for the scenario.

Estimation technique questions are usually about schedule or cost estimating, and rarely feature human resources. Part of the challenge of this question is not only knowing the various estimating techniques, but re-thinking the usual way of using them (to consider them for estimating people and roles) making it a somewhat unusual estimating question.

A25   Question 25: Answer

An organization is considering a product development project. A needs assessment and the business case have already been completed.

A management team wants the product to begin delivering business value as soon as possible.

As part of pre-project work, what should be done next?

- A) Developing a WBS that is decomposed to a level to support an MVP in the first release of the product under development
- B) Creating a list of objectives and reasons for project initiation and including them in the project business documents
- ✓ **C) Recording the need to release an MMF as part of the timeframe for benefits realization in the benefits management plan**
- D) Documenting an incremental life cycle in the project charter as the approach needed to deliver business value quickly

All answers:

A) Developing a WBS that is decomposed to a level to support an MVP in the first release of the product under development
Incorrect. The work breakdown structure (WBS) is created as a part of the Create WBS process during project planning. The scenario indicates that pre-project work is still underway. A minimum viable product (MVP) might be used to gain early feedback from a subset of customers but is not typically developed to a state that will deliver business value.

B) Creating a list of objectives and reasons for project initiation and including them in the project business documents
Incorrect. The business case should include a list of objectives and reasons for project initiation. However, the question stipulates that the business case has already been developed. Therefore, this action should have already been completed.

✓ **C) Recording the need to release an MMF as part of the timeframe for benefits realization in the benefits management plan**
Correct. The benefits management plan is created as part of pre-project work and should include a timeframe for the realization of benefits. MMF stands for minimum marketable features and represents the bare minimum of features and functionality that are required to release a product to derive business value.

D) Documenting an incremental life cycle in the project charter as the approach needed to deliver business value quickly
Incorrect. An incremental life cycle is a good strategy to support the early delivery of business value. However, the scenario stipulates that pre-project work is still being performed. The project charter would not be developed until project initiation.

Explanation:

The scenario stipulates that pre-project work is still being performed and that the needs assessment and business case have already been completed. The only other project artifact that might be developed as part of pre-project work would be the benefits management plan. The benefits management plan should include target benefits and a timeframe for realizing the benefits. The minimum marketable features (MMF) represent the bare minimum of features and functionality that are required to release a product to derive business value. Thus the release of the MMF would be the earliest that business value could be derived from the project. Therefore, of the available options, the best alternative would be to record the release of the MMF as part of the timeframe for benefits realization in the benefits management plan.

Note that even if one is not familiar with the term MMF, the question can still be answered by knowing what activities are typically carried out as part of pre-project work, by understanding what the benefits management plan includes, or by just eliminating choices that represent less plausible answers.

References:

A Guide to the Project Management Body of Knowledge, (*PMBOK® Guide*) – Sixth Edition, Project Management Institute Inc., 2017, Page(s) 29-30, 33

Agile Practice Guide – First Edition, Project Management Institute Inc, 2018, Page(s) 23

Lean-Agile Software Development, Alan Shalloway, Guy Beaver, James R. Trott, 2010, The Product Company

https://www.agilealliance.org/glossary/mmf/

Did you get it right?

Here are some reasons why people get this question wrong.

- The four choices are very similar, so test takers may choose the incorrect one.
- They aren't clear on the difference between pre-project work and the Initiating stage of a project. The team would not create the WBS or have a charter as part of pre-project work. The word 'initiating' in English actually suggests 'pre-project' (because it sounds like the earliest work on the project) but that is not how the *PMBOK® Guide* defines 'initiating'.
- The scenario suggests iterative/incremental/MVP/MMF, so the test taker right away realizes they have to choose between MVP and MMF when they first look at the four choices – and both could arguably fit the question.
- It's a hybrid scenario, which always makes a question more challenging.

Being able to answer this question successfully hinges on understanding what MVP and MMF mean.

More on MVP/MMF

To get this answer right, you have to analyze the details in choices A and C to see if either matches the question better, and then on top of that see if that is still true based on whether you're going for the MVP or the MMF choice.

There is some discrepancy among agile experts about MVP and MMF and whether the terms can be used interchangeably. It's good to know that some terms are not exactly binary, and MVP and MMF are two such terms.

One source makes a big distinction; another uses them interchangeably. The lesson here is that the PMP exam officially draws on ten sources, not only the *PMBOK® Guide* and the Agile Practice Guide.

The difference between terms like MVP and MMF can be partly dependent on which source the question writer is working from when they write the question, so be flexible if you see two very similar terms offered in two different choices.

Question 26: Answer

A26

You plan a project where you need several external contractors to complete the project deliverables. In past projects, internal developers have had disruptive personality conflicts with contractors. Therefore, before making any long-term commitments, you want to ensure that the contractors are a good fit for your corporate culture and will work well with the internal team.

What is your best course of action?

    A) Send potential contractors to team building workshops

✓ **B) Conduct a trial engagement with several potential contractors for initial deliverables**

    C) Cover the team charter with the contractors before engaging their services

    D) Organize a meet and greet with potential contractors and the development team

All answers:

    A) Send potential contractors to team building workshops
       Incorrect. While team-building workshops may enhance social relations among team members, it probably would be more effective and useful to send actual teams to team building activities and training as part of the Develop Team process rather than potential contractors. In addition, it may not be economically feasible to send all potential contractors to these workshops.

☑ **B) Conduct a trial engagement with several potential contractors for initial deliverables**

Correct. Conducting a trial engagement will engage several candidate sellers for initial deliverables and work products on a paid basis before making the full commitment to a larger portion of the project scope.

C) Cover the team charter with the contractors before engaging their services

Incorrect. Covering the team charter with the contractors may provide some future benefits in avoiding conflict. However, the team charter is most effective when those subjected to its terms have input into its development. Additionally, just covering the team charter with the contractors will not provide any insight into how the contractors will interact with the company's employees.

D) Organize a meet and greet with potential contractors and the development team

Incorrect. Holding a meet and greet is a good idea as it will allow potential contractors and internal employees an opportunity to interact in a social setting. However, a meet and greet will not provide an opportunity to evaluate how the employees will get along with the contractors in an actual work environment.

Explanation:

The question suggests that you are developing the procurement management plan as part of the Plan Procurement Management process. Trial engagements are one of the trends and emerging practices in procurement management. Conducting a trial engagement will involve several candidate sellers for initial deliverables and work products on a paid basis before making the full commitment to a larger portion of the project scope. This engagement may help accelerate momentum by allowing the buyer to evaluate potential providers, while simultaneously making progress on project work.

The incorrect answer choices are all good ideas that should be incorporated into the procurement management plan. However, prospective PMP aspirants should always select the 'best' answer among the available options. Conducting a trial engagement is the best course of action in this scenario.

Reference:

A Guide to the Project Management Body of Knowledge, (*PMBOK® Guide*) – Sixth Edition, Project Management Institute Inc., 2017, Page(s) 464

Did you get it right?

This is a very tough question because both B and D are good choices.

Here are some reasons why a test taker might not have chosen B as the correct answer.

- It sounds like a waste of time and money to hire several vendors, and then wind up cutting back to only one.
- It also sounds like a waste to go through several contract processes with several vendors, and then in the end, wind up working with one vendor.
- It could cause bad feelings between the performing organization and the vendors who end up getting rejected after they first do work for them.
- It could be a lot of effort if you have to manage several contractors at the same time, compared to only one, and information about the project might be lost in the process. For example, in a scenario like this, would you be getting lessons learned from all the activities being worked on by all the vendors? And would you have the resources to properly manage the several vendors equally well? Would there be confidentiality issues, where one vendor might see what another vendor was doing since they both are working on the same project?

In addition, with the modern trend toward agile and hybrid methods, especially standup meetings and retrospectives, choice B doesn't seem practical. You would be very unlikely to hold a morning standup with representatives from multiple vendors in the room.

They would very likely make it more about winning the competition, and less about the project success, and this goes against the goal of the morning standup with its three questions strictly geared to project success.

It's even more unlikely that you could have proper retros if you included representatives from multiple vendors. The temptation for the vendors to misuse the retro as a vehicle to compete and even finger-point would be strong and inevitable, and this would not serve the greater good of the project.

Therefore, you would likely need to conduct the standups and retros without the vendors present, and this might mean sacrificing the effectiveness of the meetings for the sake of allowing multiple vendors to work on the beginning of the project per the scenario.

All of this could be going through a test taker's head, leading them away from the correct answer.

However, the *PMBOK® Guide* is clear that choice B is the preferred route forward. Someone who doesn't know that this method is in the *PMBOK® Guide* might view this as not such a great idea, and prefer choice D, which also fits the bill, and would likely also work. This is another example of where it's important to know what's in the *PMBOK® Guide*, regardless of what tailored decision you would make for your own project.

The other two responses where people often make mistakes are incorrectly choosing the team charter. Let's look at why that might have looked right at first glance and why you shouldn't have chosen it.

More on team charters

On paper, this sounds like a good choice: talk about the charter with the vendors so they end up very well versed in what the project requires. Test takers may feel this will lead to project success, including personal interactions between the team and the contractors.

However, that kind of analytical thinking leaves out the human element, which makes choices B and D more likely to ensure that the vendors will be the right compatibility match with the team.

C might look like an efficient choice, but project managers with strong people skills would most likely immediately gravitate to other choices. Project managers with a tendency to prioritize facts over emotional intelligence may lean towards the incorrect choice here.

Take the time to think about what your prejudices, biases, and leanings might be, based on your background, experience, sector. As you've been doing practice questions, have your experience-based biases cost you any test-points? And if so, think about how to be open-minded and avoid letting them cause you to get any wrong on the test.

Question 27: Answer

During project execution, a change request is submitted to include a new set of high-priority requirements to the product. The change requires an increase in the project scope and budget. The change request is approved, and the project manager updates the document that will be used in the Control Scope process to detect any deviation in the agreed-upon scope.

Which of the following documents did the project manager update?

- ☑ **A) Requirements documentation**
- B) Requirements traceability matrix
- C) Scope management plan
- D) Configuration management plan

All answers:

- ☑ **A) Requirements documentation**
  Correct. The requirements documentation is a description of how

individual requirements meet the business need for the project. The requirements documentation is used as an input to the Control Scope process to detect any deviation in the agreed-upon scope.

B) Requirements traceability matrix
Incorrect. The requirements traceability matrix is a grid that links the product requirements from their origin to the deliverables that satisfy them. The requirements traceability matrix, which is an input to the Control Scope process, should be updated to reflect the new product features.

However, as it pertains to the Control Scope process, a deviation from the project scope must first be identified before the impact of the deviation can be assessed. The requirements documentation is used first to detect any deviation in the agreed-upon scope. The requirements traceability matrix is later used to determine potential impact of the change or deviation from the scope baseline.

C) Scope management plan
Incorrect. The scope management plan details how the scope is defined, developed, monitored, controlled, and validated. This plan does not describe what the scope is. It is unlikely that the scope management plan would need to be updated as a result of the situation described in the scenario. Additionally, the question is asking about a project document, while this answer choice represents a component of the project management plan.

D) Configuration management plan
Incorrect. The configuration management plan describes how to identify and account for project artifacts under configuration control, and how to record and report changes to them. No information presented in the question suggests that changes are required to project artifacts under configuration control. Additionally, the question is asking about a project document, while this answer choice represents a component of the project management plan.

Explanation:
The question describes a situation where new high-priority requirements are being added to the project's scope. The addition of these requirements necessitates updates to the requirements documentation and the requirements traceability matrix. The requirements documentation is a description of how individual requirements meet the business need for the project. The requirements traceability matrix is a grid that links product requirements from their origin to the deliverables that satisfy them.

Although both the requirements documentation and the requirements traceability matrix are inputs to the Control Scope process, the requirements documentation is used to detect any deviation to the agreed-upon scope; whereas, the requirements traceability matrix helps to determine the impact of any change or deviation from the scope baseline. As it pertains to the Control Scope process, a deviation from the project scope must first be identified before the impact of the deviation can be assessed. Therefore, of the available options, updating the requirements documentation is what should be done first.

Reference:
A Guide to the Project Management Body of Knowledge, (*PMBOK® Guide*) – Sixth Edition, Project Management Institute Inc., 2017, Page(s) 169, 147-148

Did you get it right?

The toughest thing about this question is that two of the choices, the requirements documentation and the requirements traceability matrix, would both be updated – and they are both inputs to the Control Scope Process. That makes both those choices sound good.

Making this one even tougher is that *PMBOK® Guide* (page 167) also lists the configuration management plan as an input to the Control Scope process, making D seem like it might be correct also.

Using the so-called rule of spotting the answer that looks different to the others, some test takers might think that since this one (D) sounds different than the other three, that maybe makes it the best of the three. However, as we saw with question 24, that's not a reliable rule!

More on the scope management plan

The scope management plan also sounds like a possible solution at first glance, for two reasons.

First, the question might lead you to look for a scope document instead of a requirements document because it is asking for a document that will be used in the Control Scope process. That implies that all the scope planning processes are already completed, so you may conclude that you should be looking for an output of those processes, created later at the end of scope planning.

Second, the scope management plan sounds like scope statement, and many students have trouble with this pair, because they sound very similar. They are created sequentially:

- The scope management plan by the Plan Scope Management process, and then;
- The scope statement, by the Define Scope Process.

If 'scope statement' was a choice, it might be a better response than choice A, because both would be correct, the scope statement would be created later, and therefore that might make it the preferred document for the Control Scope process.

However, you can only choose from the options presented!

Question 28: Answer

A conflict between the project manager and the team has been going for a while. The conflict negatively impacts the team's morale and jeopardizes the project's goals. To find a suitable resolution technique, the project manager maps the desire to satisfy the concerns of the parties on the chart below. Based on the map, the project manager decides to smooth the conflict.

Where did the project manager most likely map the desire to satisfy the team members' concerns vs. the desire to satisfy his/her own concerns?

(On the real PMP exam you may be asked to provide your answer by clicking the correct area in the image. But here in this book, we are asking you to select the answer below.)

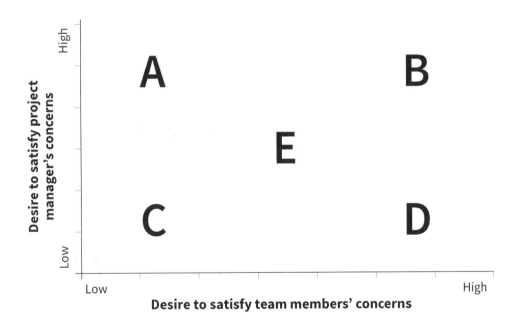

A) A
B) B
C) C
☑ **D) D**
E) E

All answers:

A) A

Incorrect. Area A represents a low desire to satisfy team members' concerns but a high desire to satisfy the project manager's own concerns. From the project manager's perspective, this would be a force/direct technique, in which the project manager would push his/her viewpoint at the expense of the team, offering a win-lose solution. In the scenario described, the project manager decides to smooth the conflict, making this choice an incorrect answer.

B) B

Incorrect. Area B represents a high desire to satisfy team members' concerns as well as a high desire to satisfy the project manager's own concerns. From the project manager's perspective, this would be a collaborate/problem-solve technique, in which multiple viewpoints and insights from different perspectives are incorporated. This approach typically results in a win-win situation. In the scenario described, the project manager decides to smooth the conflict, making this choice an incorrect answer.

C) C

Incorrect. Area C represents a low desire to satisfy team members' concerns as well as a low desire to satisfy the project manager's own concerns. From the project manager's perspective, this would be an avoid/withdraw technique, in which parties retreat from an actual or potential conflict situation, postponing the issue to be better prepared or to be resolved by others. In the scenario described, the project manager decides to smooth the conflict, making this choice an incorrect answer.

✓ **D) D**

Correct. Area D represents a high desire to satisfy team members' concerns but a low desire to satisfy the project manager's own concerns. From the project manager's perspective, this would be a smooth/accommodate technique in which one party concedes its position to the need of the other party to maintain harmony and relationships. In the scenario described, the project manager selected smoothing as the conflict resolution approach, implying he/she has decided to concede his/her position to the needs of the team to maintain harmony and relationships, making this choice the best answer to the question asked.

E) E

Incorrect. Area E represents a moderate desire to satisfy team members' concerns as well as a moderate desire to satisfy the project manager's own concerns. From the project manager's perspective, this would be a compromise/reconcile technique, in which parties search for solutions that bring some degree of satisfaction to all those involved in the conflict. Since each party moderately yields to the other side, this technique only temporarily or partially resolves the conflict and often results in a lose-lose situation. In the scenario described, the project manager decides to smooth the conflict, making this choice an incorrect answer.

Explanation:

Conflict is inevitable on any project. Therefore, conflict management is one of the most important interpersonal and team skills that project managers have to master. The success of project managers in managing their project teams often depends on their ability to resolve conflict. In the scenario described, the conflict is between the project manager and the team. The conflict is at the level that negatively impacts the team's morale and jeopardizes the project's goals.

However, selecting the appropriate conflict resolution technique depends on the project manager and the circumstances surrounding the conflict. Under different circumstances, different project managers may use different conflict resolution methods. Factors that influence these methods include the importance and intensity of the conflict, time pressure for resolving the conflict, relative power of the people involved in the conflict, importance of maintaining a good relationship, motivation to resolve conflict on a long-term or short-term basis, etc.

There are five general techniques for resolving conflict: withdrawal/avoiding, smoothing/accommodating, compromising/reconciling, forcing/directing, collaborating/problem-solving. In the scenario, the project manager decides to smooth the conflict. There is not enough information in the scenario to determine whether the project manager's decision was right or wrong. However, this information is not required to answer the question correctly. All that is needed to select the correct answer is to understand the various degrees of desire to satisfy the concerns of the parties involved in the conflict and map the desire to the technique described in the scenario, keeping in mind that the scenario is presented from the project manager's perspective.

References:
A Guide to the Project Management Body of Knowledge, (*PMBOK® Guide*) – Sixth Edition, Project Management Institute Inc., 2017, Page(s) 349

https://www.pmi.org/learning/library/project-management-organizational-conflict-resolution-2035

Did you get it right?

Here are some reasons why test takers get this question wrong:

- They don't understand exactly what the *PMBOK® Guide* means by smoothing for this scenario, and they misinterpret the term to mean to end the conflict. That's a reasonable assumption because in colloquial English that's what smoothing usually means: 'smooth it over.'
- They thought it was a better choice to make the solution more win-win, making the team-members happy and solving the conflict, and also making themselves happy at the same time, because their role as the manager entitles them to a say in the outcome.
- They recall that the *PMBOK® Guide* emphasizes going for a win-win in contract negotiations.
- They understand that the scenario in this question has an urgency to hurry up and solve the issue, improve the team's morale, and get the team productive asap, leading them to conclude that a win-win is the best approach for everyone.

If you found this question tough, refresh the conflict management approaches.

Question 29: Answer

As the project manager, you are in the process of developing a draft of a document that authorizes a new software development project. You have reviewed the agreements and both business documents.

What else should be done as part of this process?

- A) Identify stakeholders and prepare the stakeholder register
- ✓ **B) Study the governance functions and processes to provide guidance and decision making**
- C) Update the business documents to correct any errors
- D) Review the benefits management plan

All answers:

- A) Identify stakeholders and prepare the stakeholder register
  Incorrect. The question implies that you, as the project manager, are conducting the Develop Project Charter process. The stakeholder register is developed during the Identify Stakeholders process and not the Develop Project Charter process.

- ✓ **B) Study the governance functions and processes to provide guidance and decision making**
  Correct. The project governance framework is part of the organizational process assets (OPA), which serve as an input into the Develop Project Charter process.

C) Update the business documents to correct any errors
Incorrect. The project manager may make recommendations but does not update or modify the business documents since they are not project documents.

D) Review the benefits management plan
Incorrect. The benefits management plan and business case comprise the business documents, and the question states that these documents have already been reviewed.

Explanation:

The scenario describes a project manager who is developing a draft of the project charter, implying the Develop Project Charter process is carried out. One of the typical activities performed while developing the charter is to review organizational process assets (OPAs), which may influence this process. One of the OPAs is the project governance framework which often provides information about the governance functions, processes, that are important when making decisions that are relevant to the project charter.

One may argue that a stakeholder register can be created at the same time the project charter is developed and approved. While that's true, the question is asking to select the answer choice that represents an action performed 'during this process'. Since the scenario describes the Develop Project Charter process, any action that is associated with this process would be a better option than an action associated with another process, even if that process can be done in parallel with the one described in the scenario.

Therefore, as we always recommend selecting the best answer of those provided, studying the governance functions and processes to provide guidance and decision making is a better answer choice than identifying stakeholders and preparing the stakeholder register since the former is associated with the inputs to the Develop Project Charter process while the latter is not even part of this process.

Reference:
A Guide to the Project Management Body of Knowledge, (*PMBOK® Guide*) – Sixth Edition, Project Management Institute Inc., 2017, Page(s) 79, 545

Did you get it right?

The question is clearly about developing a project charter, even though it doesn't explicitly say so. Here are some reasons why test takers get this question wrong.

- The three incorrect choices are all good responses! They all sound reasonable at first glance.

- They might not consider the correct answer as something that falls into the process of developing the project charter.
- They might not have spent enough time studying governance functions, or consider that these are important.

More on the project charter

When creating the Project Charter, it's important to study the governance functions for the company to help guide the project, and make sure it is going to be executed in line with the company's policies, procedures and rules (and not simply creating the deliverables).

If choice B was simplified to say, "Study the OPAs and EEFs," for example, that would make it much easier. But these are tricky questions for a reason!

A30 Question 30: Answer

During project execution, the project manager learns of a new government regulation that will impact her commercial building construction project. Specifically, regulatory compliance will now require the addition of a redundant fire suppression system. This risk had been identified during initial project planning, and appropriate contingency reserves were allocated. The project manager submits a change request, which is subsequently approved.

Which of the following project artifacts will most likely be updated as a result of this regulatory change? (Choose four.)

- A) Cost baseline
- ✓ **B) Scope baseline**
- ✓ **C) Risk register**
- D) Change management plan
- ✓ **E) Activity list**
- F) Configuration management plan
- ✓ **G) Change log**

All answers:

- A) Cost baseline
  Incorrect. The question states that adequate contingency reserves were allocated to address the risk of adding a redundant fire suppression system. Since contingency reserves are already included in the cost baseline, a change to the cost baseline should not be necessary.

- ✓ **B) Scope baseline**
  Correct. Compliance with the new regulation will require the addition of a redundant fire suppression system, which represents an increase in the project scope. The scope baseline will need to be revised to include the additional scope.

☑ **C) Risk register**

Correct. The risk register typically includes risk status as a component. Since the revised regulation represents a realized risk, at a minimum, the risk status will need to be updated in this scenario.

D) Change management plan

Incorrect. The change management plan establishes the change control board, documents the extent of its authority, and describes how the change control system will be implemented. The change management plan will be implemented in this scenario, but there is no indication that the change management plan itself will need to be revised.

☑ **E) Activity list**

Correct. The activity list is a project document that records the activity description, activity identifier, and a detailed description of the scope of work. All of the activities associated with the addition of the redundant fire suppression system will need to be included in the activity list.

F) Configuration management plan

Incorrect. The configuration management plan is the component of the project management plan that describes how to identify and account for project artifacts under configuration control and how to record and report changes to them. There is no indication in this scenario that the artifacts under configuration control will need to be revised.

☑ **G) Change log**

Correct. The change log is a comprehensive list of changes submitted during the project and their current status. Since a change request was submitted and approved in this scenario, the change log will need to be updated accordingly.

Explanation:

In this scenario, a regulatory change has necessitated the inclusion of redundant fire suppression system, which represents an increase in the project scope. A change to the scope baseline requires an approved change request, which was submitted and approved in this case. As with any change request, the change log will need to be updated to reflect the status of the requested change.

Since the project scope is increasing, the added scope will need to be reflected in the work breakdown structure (WBS). The lowest level of the WBS is the work package level. The work packages are further decomposed to create a project document called the activity list. The additional project scope will need to be decomposed to include the additional work packages and associated activities, which necessitates a change to the existing activity list.

Additionally, with the risk associated with the increase in project scope being identified during initial project planning (perhaps the legislation was pending approval), the risk was included in the risk register, and contingency reserves were assigned. The risk register typically includes risk status, which will need to be updated with the risk being realized.

In this scenario, the aforementioned contingency reserves should address the impact on the cost and schedule of the project. Implementing an approved risk response does not require change management. One might argue that the risk response plan could also include changes to the scope baseline, but there is no information presented in the question to suggest this was the case. Therefore, while the cost and schedule baseline are not likely to need to be updated, the scope baseline will need to be revised.

It should also be noted that the correct answers are not intended to be an exhaustive list of project artifacts that will likely need to be updated in this scenario. Additional elements of the project management plan, project schedule, activity attributes, lessons learned register, physical resource assignments, project team assignments, etc. will likely need to be revised as well. This scenario demonstrated the domino effect that can occur when changes are required to be made when a project is already in execution.

Reference:
A Guide to the Project Management Body of Knowledge, (*PMBOK® Guide*) – Sixth Edition, Project Management Institute Inc., 2017, Page(s) 89, 120, 398, 417, 451-452

Did you get it right?
First, this one is tough because questions that ask you to select all that apply are always challenging, and take a lot more time to respond to than multiple choice.

What makes this question especially hard is that all the choices here sound possible at first. Here are some reasons why each of the choices could have some merit, and tips for making the right choice.

Cost baseline
It's an incorrect choice in the context of this question but it looks like it easily could be correct.

It is logical to assume that more scope equates to more money, and it's an exception to this rule that more scope does not mean more money here. It is going to cost more money to add the new system. And just because the money has already been allocated in the original cost baseline, it still is the case that the project will cost more money than it would have if the new system had not been added.

It's far from obvious that the cost baseline will not need to be updated to reflect the additional cost of the extra system. However, a lesson learned here is that adding extra scope does not necessarily require a change to the cost baseline, even though that will seem counter-intuitive to some test takers.

Scope baseline
This one is easy – it's fairly obvious to correctly reason that a change to the scope will mean a change to the scope baseline, since the redundant system needs to be planned into all three components of the Scope Baseline.

Risk register
This one is a correct choice, but in some ways it looks like an incorrect choice, because from what the question says, you might conclude that risk management was already done for this risk and that no more activity was needed for it. After all, it was already added to the risk register and budgeted for with contingency reserves.

If this risk had not been already identified, and contingency reserves had not already been allocated, that might be two big reasons that the risk register would need to be updated.

Change management plan
The question specifically mentions the action of a change request and approval. If you only read the question quickly, that might lead you to conclude that this was a viable choice.

However, the change log is the better change-related choice of the two. Some test takers might choose both D and G because they are both about change management.

Project managers who do not work with an extensive project management plan (the *PMBOK® Guide* way) often have a hard time with the concept of all the subcomponents of the project management plan. They don't understand the need for all those plans (change, risk, cost, schedule, scope, resource, etc.), so they don't understand why a change request would not mean a change to the change management plan, and they might select this response incorrectly.

Activity list
This one is easy. If you are adding the redundant system, the activities to add it must be added to the project schedule.

Configuration management plan
The configuration management plan describes how changes will be made in a controlled way, but won't need to change as a result of this scenario. However, it is related to change, and test takers who don't fully understand configuration management may be confused by its presence in the list.

Change log

The wording of this choice makes it tricky for two reasons. First, the question says that a change request was already submitted, so some test takers might think that no further change-related action is needed. Second, the grammar of the phrase "is subsequently approved" in the question is a little ambiguous.

Was the change already approved, and possibly no longer requiring an update to the change log? Or does the wording mean that it got approved later in time, after the scenario of the question, and therefore the change log will need to be approved later once the approval takes place.

None of the choices can be quickly eliminated with this question. Many test takers are used to the technique of eliminating two responses and then picking the best of the remaining options. That approach won't work so well on questions that ask you to select several correct responses.

This type of question is tricky because it requires several decisions, not just one, and they take longer than questions that simply ask you to select a single response.

Be ready to spend more time on this type when you see it and be prepared to put special effort into them when you encounter them. Take notes on these specifically to help you with this type of question on your test day.

A31 Question 31: Answer

An agile team is using a Kanban board to manage their workflow. The work in progress limits (WIP) are indicated at the header of each column. The team reviews the board during the daily standup meeting to coordinate their activities for the day.

Which of the following actions might the team consider taking? (Choose three.)

To Do (eight)	Development (four)	Integration (two)	Testing (two)	Acceptance (three)	Deploy to Production
User story 21	User story 19	User story 17	User story 15	User story 11	User story 1
User story 22	User story 20	User story 18	User story 16	User story 12	User story 2
User story 23				User story 13	User story 3
User story 24					User story 4
User story 25					User story 5
User story 26					User story 6
User story 27					User story 7
User story 28					User story 8
					User story 9
					User story 10

A) Add another user story from the backlog to the 'To Do' column

✓ **B) Swap a user story from the 'To Do' column with a user story from the backlog**

✓ **C) Pull an item from the 'To Do' column to begin development work**

D) Assuming integration for user story 17 is complete, begin its testing

E) Deploy user story 16 to production since that column does not have WIP limits

✓ **F) Gain acceptance for user story 13 and deploy it to production**

All answers:

A) Add another user story from the backlog to the 'To Do' column
Incorrect. The Kanban board indicates that there are eight user stories in the 'To Do' column with a work in progress (WIP) limit of eight. Since the WIP limit of the 'To Do' column has been reached, no other user stories can be added to this column at this point.

✓ **B) Swap a user story from the 'To Do' column with a user story from the backlog**
Correct. Although the work in progress (WIP) limit has been reached for the 'To Do' column, swapping a user story from the backlog is an option as this action would not affect the WIP limit. This action can be done in coordination with the product owner to ensure the prioritization order of the user stories is maintained.

✓ **C) Pull an item from the 'To Do' column to begin development work**
Correct. The 'Development' column currently has two user stories with a work in progress (WIP) limit of four. Therefore, the project team can consider moving a user story from the 'To Do' column into development.

D) Assuming integration for user story 17 is complete, begin its testing
Incorrect. Even if integration for user story 17 is complete, the user story is not eligible for testing because the 'Testing' column has already reached its work in progress (WIP) limit.

E) Deploy user story 16 to production since that column does not have WIP limits
Incorrect. The 'Deploy to Production' column does not have an associated work in progress limit (WIP). However, once testing has been completed, the user story still needs to receive final approval (to be accepted) before it can be deployed into production.

✓ **F) Gain acceptance for user story 13 and deploy it to production**
Correct. The 'Deploy to Production' column does not have an associated work in progress limit (WIP). Therefore, once the user story has been accepted, it can then be deployed into production.

Explanation:

A common practice when employing the Kanban method is to establish a work in progress (WIP) limit for each stage of work represented by the columns on the Kanban board. The WIP limits will help identify bottlenecks and improve throughput. When WIP limits are assigned to a stage of work, that number is recorded in the header with the appropriate column of the Kanban board/ table.

In the scenario, only the 'Development' and 'Deploy to Production' columns have not reached their WIP limits and are available to accept additional work. The correct answers represent actions that are viable options based on the established WIP limits.

References:

Agile Practice Guide – First Edition, Project Management Institute Inc, 2018, Page(s) 65-66, 105

Kanban – Successful Evolutionary Change for Your Technology Business, David J. Anderson, 2010, Setting Work-in-Progress Limits

Did you get it right?

A good way to describe this question is: "easy when you know how."

Knowing several fundamental Kanban principles is essential to getting this one right, especially when the test taker has to select three out of six responses. Here's what you need to know:

- The basic idea of the Kanban board
- The 'pull' concept in Kanban
- The flow from left-to-right on the board, and how no story can skip over a column (which is what invalidates choice E, but which validates choice F)
- The concept of limits on each column, and that the numbers at the top of each column represent the limits, and that those limits are strict and cannot be gotten around (which is what invalidates choices A and D, but validates choice C)
- How stories get from the backlog to the To Do column, and possibly back again (which validates choice B).

Understanding Scrum is not enough for the agile and hybrid questions on the test. It's tempting to think that the agile part of the exam is no big deal, or because you work in an agile environment you know enough to pass.

However, you'll need to know several agile areas (including Scrum, Kanban, Lean Agile and XP) in order to confidently face all the questions, as well as the agile mindset.

Question 32: Answer

A32

You and your project team have just completed defining the scope for your project and are now in the process of decomposing the scope statement to create the work breakdown structure (WBS). Some of the deliverables will be produced later in the project and cannot be entirely decomposed at this time.

When you have completed the process of creating the WBS, your scope baseline will include which of the following components?

- A) Project scope statement, WBS, and activity attributes
- B) Project scope statement, WBS, WBS dictionary, and activity list
- C) Project scope statement, activity list, and activity attributes
- ✓ **D) Project scope statement, work packages, and planning packages**

All answers:

A) Project scope statement, WBS, and activity attributes
Incorrect. The project scope statement and WBS are components of the scope baseline, which is the main output from the Create WBS process described in the scenario. Activity attributes are an output from the Define Activities process.

B) Project scope statement, WBS, WBS dictionary, and activity list
Incorrect. The project scope statement, WBS, and WBS dictionary are components of the scope baseline, which is the main output from the Create WBS process described in the scenario. The activity list is an output from the Define Activities process.

C) Project scope statement, activity list, and activity attributes
Incorrect. The activity list and activity attributes are outputs of the Define Activities process, while the question describes the Create WBS process.

✓ **D) Project scope statement, work packages, and planning packages**
Correct. Components of the scope baseline include the project scope statement, WBS, work packages, planning packages, and WBS dictionary. While this answer choice is incomplete, of the choices provided, it is still the best answer to the question asked.

Explanation:

The output of the Create WBS process is the approved version of the scope baseline which includes a scope statement, WBS, work package, planning package, and WBS dictionary. Typically, one thinks of a scope baseline as the scope statement, WBS, and WBS dictionary. But when asked about scope baseline components, one must include the work packages and planning packages which provide the structure for the control accounts. Scope, budget, and schedule are integrated and used for performance measurement at management control points called control accounts which are noted in the WBS. Therefore, the answer that included the work package and planning package is correct.

Note, the correct answer is incomplete. It includes only some of the components of the scope baseline. However, the incorrect answer choices contain components that are not part of the scope baseline at all. Therefore, as we always recommend, of the options provided, select the one that is better than the others even if that option is not an ideal/perfect answer or the answer you would like to see as the correct one.

Reference:
A Guide to the Project Management Body of Knowledge, (*PMBOK® Guide*) – Sixth Edition, Project Management Institute Inc., 2017, Page(s) 161-162

Did you get it right?
The biggest difficulty of this one is that the definition of the scope baseline is very clearly three components:

- Scope statement
- WBS
- WBS dictionary

but none of the four choices includes all three of the above components.

If you know the correct definition of the scope baseline, you would be looking for exactly the above but not finding them in any of the four choices.

Since that triple is not one of the four choices, you have to search for the next closest thing, and settle for an ambiguous choice as the correct answer.

Let's review why each of the answer choices makes this a tricky question.

Project scope statement, WBS, and activity attributes
The first two are correct, but activity attributes would not have been created yet until a couple of processes later in the Define Activities process. That makes the third component invalid for this answer.

However, a test taker might see that the first two are spot-on, and try to rationalize to themselves why this is still a pretty good answer. For example, they might reason that when the WBS work packages get further broken down, the activity attributes become part of the WBS in a way (even though not officially), so they might conclude that A is a very close answer.

Project scope statement, WBS, WBS dictionary, and activity list

All three correct answers are here, but the fourth component invalidates this choice, for the same reason as in the choice above: the activity list does not exist yet.

It gets created two steps later, in Define Activities, and each activity gets associated with its parent work package in the WBS.

In their eagerness to select the 'most right' answer, a test taker can fall into the trap of accepting an incorrect choice.

Project scope statement, activity list, and activity attributes

There is only one correct component in this choice. However, again it is a close answer, for the reasons described above.

Project scope statement, work packages, and planning packages

By the time you get to the final choice it doesn't look right! It only contains one obviously correct component of the scope baseline: the scope statement. Both of the other two parts of this choice look partly wrong, even though they are both sort of right.

Work packages are part of the WBS, which is part of the scope baseline, but they are not the entire WBS.

Planning packages are also part of the WBS, but not the entire WBS. And you might not be confident in what a planning package is.

Even if you conclude that all three of the pieces of this choice are individually correct, an important component of the scope baseline is completely missing from this choice: the WBS dictionary.

That might make you reluctant to choose choice D because, if you know what belongs in the scope baseline, choice D is clearly incomplete. You risk spending too much time on this question trying to select the most appropriate choice.

This question gives a great example of one of the kinds of ambiguity that the test taker might see on the real test, where the best answer is not 100% perfect, but it's still the best of the four.

The perfect answer is not offered, so the test taker has to be mentally tough and pick the choice that is the best. Even though it isn't perfect, don't spend too much trying to find the perfect solution.

Sometimes you simply have to pick the one that can't be considered incorrect. In this question, the best course of action is to go with incomplete choice D, over the others, which all have at least one demonstrably false thing about them. If there is something incorrect about a choice, you can usually safely eliminate it.

More on packages

It's important to know that there are three kinds of packages in a WBS, that have the following hierarchical order:

1. Control accounts
2. Planning packages
3. Work packages

Learn all of them. Many books, including the *PMBOK® Guide,* only show work packages in a diagram, and do not include the other two in the diagram. That makes it harder for students who recall the pictures from the book during the exam.

A33 Question 33: Answer

You are leading a complex project with a schedule baseline that cannot be modified due to external constraints. The scope, however, is flexible. The project deliverables are produced by three development teams that work independently from one another. The teams manage their workflow using Kanban.

Which of the following is the most effective tool for you to use to measure the project's progress?

✓ **A) Feature chart**
   B) Burndown chart
   C) Burnup chart
   D) Cumulative flow diagram

All answers:

✓ **A) Feature chart**
Correct. A feature chart can provide information about the features that have been completed, the features remaining, and the total number of features. Additionally, the feature chart can provide a visualization for the rate at which features are being developed.

   B) Burndown chart
Incorrect. Since each of the three teams is working independently, they will each perform their own relative sizing exercises and definitions for the units of measure. As a result, it will not be possible to compare teams or add velocity across teams. A burndown chart may be helpful to measure progress at the team level but not at the project level in this case.

   C) Burnup chart
Incorrect. A burnup chart might be helpful for each of the teams to use to measure their progress but will not be useful to measure the progress of the project. Since each time will likely define their units of

measure differently, you, as the project manager, will not be able to build a meaningful project level burnup chart.

D) Cumulative flow diagram

Incorrect. Although the cumulative flow diagram could provide some useful information about the progress of the project, the cumulative flow diagram is designed to break down work in progress across a Kanban board rather than measure the project's progress.

Explanation:

The question indicates that the project has a schedule baseline, and the development teams are using Kanban, which suggests that the project is undertaken using a hybrid method. According to the scenario, the project end date is fixed, but the scope is variable, which makes scheduling and progress reporting with typical waterfall methods problematic. Additionally, the question indicates that each of the three project teams is working independently. Both of these factors introduce complications for measuring the overall project's progress.

One way of addressing the progress reporting issues associated with a project with variable scope and independent project teams is to use a feature chart. A feature chart uses the number of features rather than story points, so there is a commonality between the project teams. The individual teams might use burn charts to measure their progress, but since it's likely that each team will define their units of measure differently, the burn charts cannot be combined into a meaningful project burn chart.

A feature chart can provide a visual aid for understanding the number of features that have been completed as well as the rate of feature development over time across the project teams. Therefore, a feature chart would be an ideal tool to use in the circumstances outlined in the scenario.

References:

Agile Practice Guide – First Edition, Project Management Institute Inc, 2018, Page(s) 66-67

Lean-Agile Software Development, Achieving Enterprise Agility, Alan Shalloway, Guy Beaver, James R. Trott, 2010, Establishing Clear Line of Sight

Did you get it right?

This is an extremely difficult question for several reasons. Let's look at the different types of charts to help you understand more about what this question is asking.

Feature Charts

Feature charts are much less commonly seen in books on agile, and also less often-used on real projects than the more common burndown and burnup charts.

Every book on project management nowadays includes burndown charts, and many also include burnup charts, whereas fewer books include illustrations of feature charts.

The test taker's natural reaction to this question may be to think of the others first, and maybe not feature charts at all if they are unfamiliar with them.

The example of a feature chart in the Agile Practice Guide looks like a burnup chart, and is actually called a feature burnup/burndown chart (check out page 67).

As it's in the category of burnup/burndown charts, you have to know that a feature chart is a specific type of burnup/burndown chart, which makes the feature chart a better answer as it is more specific.

The Agile Practice Guide does use the term feature chart by itself in the index.

Burndown Charts

At first reading, burndown charts may look like the correct answer. In books, burndown charts are shown with multiple lines, e.g. planned work versus completed work versus actual cost versus planned cost.

If a burndown chart could accurately show several lines for several projects, that would make it a perfect chart for this scenario.

If faced with this question, a test taker might recall seeing a burndown chart in a book with multiple lines and select this response. It would require a lot of thought to remember that burndown charts can show multiple lines, but then also to figure out on-the-fly that those multiple lines are not accurately used to compare the progress of different teams, because the teams use different sizing and therefore their velocities are apples-to-orange comparisons.

However, in the real world, many teams would use burndown charts for this scenario. Even though it's imperfect as a solution because different teams use different sizing methods. A test taker who has used or seen these charts on projects for this kind of scenario may be tempted to select this choice, unless they also had hands-on experience with feature charts and could appreciate the difference about why feature charts are more accurate here.

Burnup Charts

Burndown and burnup charts are so similar that people who are used to burnup more than burndown would be likely to select burnup for the same reasons as above that others would select burndown. Most books describe them as 'about the same, but in the opposite direction' and more a visual difference than a qualitative difference in what they show.

Cumulative Flow Diagrams

For many people, CFD are the most difficult to understand of the four diagrams in the answer choices.

Where many people find burndown and burnup charts immediately clear, CFDs may have to be studied closely to figure out what they are showing.

Cumulative flow diagrams usually show more than one element, such as a range of different features, so test takers with a fair understanding of CFD might select this response. You'd need a strong understanding of both cumulative flow diagrams and feature charts.

This question is really difficult, but it shows that you need to know all of these charts well, and many more besides. Some questions will simply ask you to identify a chart, but in this scenario, you have to figure out which is the most appropriate choice.

Question 34: Answer

A34

To develop an appropriate approach and plan for project communication activities, the project manager identifies several project artifacts.

What relevant information can the project manager obtain from each project artifact to begin the process? (In your exam, on a question like this you would be asked to drag and drop the items from right to left. In this book, please arrange the answer choices in the correct order.)

Answer choices	Answers
Project charter	
Stakeholder register	
Enterprise environmental factors	
Organizational process assets	
Project management plan	

- Communications activities with stakeholders
- The list of key project stakeholders
- Management strategies to engage stakeholders
- Geographic distribution of resources
- Policies and procedures for social media

Answers:

Answer choices	Answers (correct order)
Project charter	**The list of key project stakeholders**
Stakeholder register	**Communications activities with stakeholders**
Enterprise environmental factors	**Geographic distribution of resources**
Organizational process assets	**Policies and procedures for social media**
Project management plan	**Management strategies to engage stakeholders**

Explanation:

Developing an appropriate approach and planning for project communications activities is the definition of the Plan Communications Management process. The main output from this process is the communications management plan. The project charter, stakeholder register, enterprise environmental factors, organizational process assets, and project management plan (among others) are all inputs to this process.

The project charter is a document issued by the project initiator or sponsor that formally authorizes the existence of a project. The charter identifies the key project stakeholders. Note that the stakeholder register contains a more comprehensive list of stakeholders that would include the key stakeholders; however, since the answer choice specifies 'key' stakeholders, the project charter is a better answer choice.

The stakeholder register is a project document that includes the identification, assessment, and classification of project stakeholders. This information can be used to help plan communication activities that would be appropriate for these stakeholders.

Enterprise environmental factors are conditions, not under the immediate control of the project team, that influence, constrain, or direct the project. The geographic distribution of facilities and resources are among the enterprise environmental factors that may impact how communications will be planned and managed. For example, the location of human resources may necessitate the need for virtual communication tools.

Organizational process assets are plans, processes, policies, procedures, and knowledge bases that are specific to and used by the performing organization. The organization's policies and procedures will provide boundaries for the acceptable use of social media, which may need to be incorporated into the communications management plan.

The stakeholder engagement plan is one of the project management plan's components that serve as an input to the Plan Communications Management process implied by the scenario. The stakeholder engagement plan identifies the management strategies required to effectively engage stakeholders.

Reference:
A Guide to the Project Management Body of Knowledge, (*PMBOK® Guide*) – Sixth Edition, Project Management Institute Inc., 2017, Page(s) 368-369

Did you get it right?

This is a hard question because it's always a lot of work with having to analyze two columns of data, with five elements in each column.

Here are some reasons why test takers get this question wrong.

- They are caught out by 'stakeholder register' as it sounds almost like a perfect definition of that document, except for the word 'key'. The charter has a list of key stakeholders, whereas the stakeholder register has a more complete list of all stakeholders. Another difference is that the Charter, once created, is set in stone, whereas the stakeholder register is a living document that is continuously updated as new stakeholders are added and some are removed from the list as the project evolves.
- Three boxes from the right column include the word 'stakeholder(s)', while the left column has only one box with that word: 'stakeholder register'. At first glance, the stakeholder register may look like a good fit for any of the items on the right, making the match difficult.
- They see 'management strategies to engage stakeholders' and seek out 'stakeholder engagement plan' in the left column, and be disappointed as it isn't there.
- The project management plan is not specifically and exclusively all about stakeholders, so even if they see it and realize they have to consider it as a match, they likely will feel uneasy about it, since it's no more a match for stakeholder engagement plan than it would be for many other components of the project management plan.
- They are distracted by the project management plan response because they can't be sure if it's a match, and that doesn't help them use the process of elimination on the other four matches – because they might find a better match in one of the other choices.

It is often very tricky to answer questions where you have to differentiate between which response is an OPA and which is an EEF. This question makes this all the more difficult because both OPAs and EEFs are listed in the left column, but those are only two out of five in that column, and all five will have to be matched up with a term in the right column.

Adding to the difficulty of this one is that the correct match for the OPA includes the word 'policies'. A popular example for remembering EEFs is the weather – you can't build houses in Florida in September because of the potential severe seasonal hurricanes, so that's an EEF for the construction industry in Florida.

In contrast, most OPAs are things that can be held in your hand, whereas most EEFs cannot. However, 'policies' feels a little in the middle and cannot be held in your hand (especially if they aren't written down) the way the following common OPAs can, like lessons learned documentation from old projects, templates, training materials and so on.

PMI clearly considers policies to be OPAs, and that's worth remembering for the test.

A35

Question 35: Answer

A project sponsor tells the project manager that stakeholder expectations and risk thresholds have not been addressed by a particular document. Project planning cannot begin until the sponsor approves this document.

What might the project manager have neglected?

- A) Review of organizational process assets
- ☑ **B) Consideration of enterprise environmental factors**
- C) Development of a risk management plan
- D) Creation of the risk register

All answers:

A) Review of organizational process assets
Incorrect. Although organizational process assets are inputs into the development of the project charter, which is the document described in the question, stakeholder expectations and risk thresholds are not an element of the organizational process assets.

☑ **B) Consideration of enterprise environmental factors**
Correct. Stakeholder expectations and risk thresholds are part of the enterprise environmental factors and serve as an input into the development of the project charter.

C) Development of a risk management plan
Incorrect. The risk management plan is a subsidiary of the project management plan. The question implies that the project is still in the initiation stage, and the risk management plan has not been developed.

D) Creation of the risk register
Incorrect. The question indicates that the project is still in the initiation

stage. The risk register is an output of the Identify Risks process, which occurs later during project planning.

Explanation:

The question suggests that the project manager has developed a draft of the project charter, which must be reviewed and approved by the project sponsor before project planning can begin. High-level risks may be captured in the project charter and may be of particular importance if key stakeholders have low-risk tolerances.

Stakeholder expectations and risk thresholds are part of the enterprise environmental factors, which may serve as an input into the development of the project charter. Therefore, of the available answer choices, the project manager most likely did not adequately consider the enterprise environmental factors.

Reference:

A Guide to the Project Management Body of Knowledge, (*PMBOK® Guide*) – Sixth Edition, Project Management Institute Inc., 2017, Page(s) 78

Did you get it right?

This question is tough. Here are some reasons why test takers might get it wrong.

- They might think they are looking for Project Charter as the answer. It isn't in the list, so that is frustrating and it takes a few moments to reset expectations of what the question is looking for. They have to re-read the question, with the Charter in mind, but now looking at it differently knowing the charter is NOT going to be the answer, and then re-read the choices again.
- They are confused between EEFs and OPAs.
- They might be looking for Stakeholder Engagement Plan as a possible choice because the question specifically mentions Stakeholder Management and Risk Thresholds not being addressed. Besides the Charter, that would be an early document that possibly could have been a correct answer, as it addresses stakeholder engagement especially, but also might touch on the risks of ignoring key stakeholders who might have been identified early on.
- Because the question asks about specific risk thresholds, they may have jumped to the conclusion that choice C could be correct. If early risk planning had been done, the Risk Management Plan possibly could have been started, and that might include risk thresholds documented early in the planning, even though the Charter is a better choice for where the thresholds should be documented at this early stage of the project.

- They might have assumed Risk Management is being planned beyond what would be documented in the charter, because risk thresholds are mentioned, and therefore chosen the risk register as the correct response as the primary artifact for documenting risk details. However, you would not have a risk register created as early in the project as the scenario indicates.

Once you've narrowed down the choices down to either OPAs or EEFs, the choice is pretty clear.

More on EEFs and OPAs

EEFs and OPAs are often confused on questions because:

- The terms EEFs and OPAs sound similar
- Both are three-word terms, and both are commonly referred to by their three-letter acronyms
- The words 'Enterprise' in EEFs and 'Organization' in OPAs are synonyms in English
- The words 'Factors' and 'Assets' also sound somewhat similar: both end in 'S', and both are two syllable-words with the accent on the first syllable
- EEFs and OPAs are often grouped together as Inputs to many of the processes in the PMBOK
- EEFs and OPAs are ALSO often grouped together as Outputs to many of the processes in the *PMBOK® Guide*
- There are some cases where it's a bit ambiguous whether something is an EEF or an OPA.

Make sure you understand the difference between them and how they are used.

A36   Question 36: Answer

A project is plagued by various issues, such as a deteriorating team performance, cost and schedule overruns, defective deliverables, etc. The project manager is struggling to monitor and control the work and decides to use some of the data analysis techniques to identify the issues and determine the best course of action.

How can the project manager use the following techniques to identify the various issues impacting this project? (In your exam, on a question like this you would be asked to drag and drop the items from right to left. In this book, please arrange the answer choices in the correct order.)

Answer choices	Answers
Corrective actions for better performance	
Corrective actions regarding the cost	
Integrated perspective on project performance	
Identify the main reason for problems	
Forecast performance based on results	
Compare planned and actual performance	
(Not applicable)	

- Earned value analysis
- Trend analysis
- Variance analysis
- Business analysis
- Root cause analysis
- Alternatives analysis
- Cost-benefit analysis

Answers:

Answer choices	Answers (correct order)
Corrective actions for better performance	**Alternatives analysis**
Corrective actions regarding the cost	**Cost-benefit analysis**
Integrated perspective on project performance	**Earned value analysis**
Identify the main reason for problems	**Root cause analysis**
Forecast performance based on results	**Trend analysis**
Compare planned and actual performance	**Variance analysis**
(Not applicable)	**Business analysis**

Explanation:

While alternatives analysis selects a corrective action or a combination of corrective and preventive actions to implement, cost-benefit analysis determines the best corrective action when it comes to cost factors in a project that deviates from the plan. With earned value analysis, project managers will have a more integrated perspective on scope, schedule, and cost performance. Root cause analysis helps identify the main cause or causes of a problem; with trend analysis, future performance can be forecasted based on past results.

The differences between planned and actual performance are reviewed with variance analysis. In contrast, business analysis is not a technique that is typically used as part of the Monitor and Control Project Work process implied by the scenario.

Reference:
A Guide to the Project Management Body of Knowledge, (*PMBOK® Guide*) – Sixth Edition, Project Management Institute Inc., 2017, Page(s) 111

Did you get it right?

There's a lot of brain work needed for this question, to interpret what is being asked, evaluate six issues, evaluate seven analysis techniques and match them up.

Questions like this might take you a bit longer than the average exam question, so be prepared to guess and mark for review, so you can come back to it later.

All seven analysis techniques are legitimate, and they all have the word "analysis" in them, making them all blur into one a little bit for the test taker.

Most of the matches on this one are tough to do. Even the easiest one, earned value analysis, could actually match three of the choices if there weren't two more specific matches that better fit the others.

'Compare planned and actual performance' applies very much to EVM in a broad sense, but more specifically applies to variance analysis.

'Forecast performance based on results' also applies very much to EVM in a broad sense, but more specifically to trend analysis.

'Integrated perspectives on project performance' is a little vague, but would be more obviously a match for EVM if it included more specifics, like comparing results against planned cost, schedule, and deliverables for the project.

As with many PMP questions, all three of the above could be correct for EVM, so the test taker has to hang in and try to pick the best one of the three to match EVM, and look to see which of the other two are better-matched to other choices.

Making this one even more difficult is that some of the matches are not obvious matches – they somewhat fit the descriptions in the other column, but they are not the definitions of those techniques that would usually be provided in a project management book or glossary.

- Alternatives analysis would not usually be defined as 'correct actions for better performance' as it is usually used with project selection.
- Cost benefit analysis is commonly used with project selection or buy-or-build choices, in advance of a project or activity, and is not commonly used for corrective actions after-the-fact (as it is offered here as the correct match).

Be ready for out-of-the-box match-ups on questions like this, and not just the typical match for an expression. Practice this type of matching question if you find them difficult, because you will get better at them.

Question 37: Answer

All the technical work on a project has been completed, and the product has been transitioned to a support team.

What should the project manager do before the project can be closed?

- A) Issue a quality report
- B) Validate the scope
- C) Close the contracts
- ☑ **D) Measure stakeholder satisfaction**

All answers:

A) Issue a quality report
   Incorrect. The quality report typically includes all of the quality assurance issues that were managed by the team, recommendations for improvement, and the summary of findings from the Control Quality process. Quality reports are an output of the Manage Quality process and an input to the Close Project or Phase process. According to the scenario, all the technical work has been completed, and the product has been transitioned to a support team suggesting the project is in the Close Project or Phase process, not the Manage Quality process.

B) Validate the scope
   Incorrect. During the Validate Scope process, the completed project deliverables are inspected and formally accepted by the customer or relevant stakeholders. In the scenario described, the product has already been transitioned to the support team. The transitioning of the product to the support team is part of the project closure. This action suggests the scope has already been validated.

C) Close the contracts

Incorrect. While closing contracts should be done before the project can be closed, there is not enough information in the question to determine if there were any contracts on the project.

✓ **D) Measure stakeholder satisfaction**

Correct. Measuring stakeholder satisfaction is one of the activities performed during project closure.

Explanation:

Since all the technical work has been completed, and the product has been transitioned to the support group, one may assume the project is in the Close Project or Phase process. When closing a project, the project manager reviews the project management plan to ensure all project work is completed, and that the project has met its objectives. Measuring stakeholder satisfaction is one of the activities which is necessary to be performed before the administrative closure of the project can take place.

Reference:

A Guide to the Project Management Body of Knowledge, (*PMBOK® Guide*) – Sixth Edition, Project Management Institute Inc., 2017, Page(s) 123, 127

Did you get it right?

You did? Well done! It's a really tough question.

Many test takers will choose to close the contracts which seems like the most sensible choice at this point. However, there might not be contracts, which makes this choice inappropriate for all projects.

Don't make the assumption that all projects use outsourcing and contracts. They are common, but many projects are done by internal teams too.

It's really important to know the contents of the *PMBOK® Guide* for questions like this one, as the correct answer is literally written in the book.

This question is made even harder because choices A and B sound reasonable too. Let's look at those.

Issue a quality report

Although it's not correct, it does sound like a good thing to do at the end of a project. The *PMBOK® Guide* talks about elaborating the final project reports and you might assume this could include the quality report.

Validate the scope

The *PMBOK® Guide* does include a few bullets that sound like and suggest choice B is correct. It talks about confirming the delivery and formal acceptance of deliverables by the customer and confirming the formal acceptance of the Seller's work.

Like issuing a quality report, this sounds like a good thing to do at the end, if you have time to keep reviewing the final product before the project is closed.

Question 38: Answer

A38

During a software development project, developers spent two days to repair a defect that was found a day earlier. The deployment team then spent another day to deploy the fix at the customer premises.

Which of the following does this four-day period represent?

- ☑ **A) Lead time**
- B) Actual time
- C) Cycle time
- D) Response time

All answers:

- ☑ **A) Lead time**

    Correct. Lead time refers to the time required for the work item to go through the entire process. So, from the time the defect was identified, it took four days for the fix to be deployed to users.

- B) Actual time

    Incorrect. Actual time takes into consideration team members' availability. Actual time is used to determine the time required to actually complete the project tasks and commit to sprint, release, and project goals.

- C) Cycle time

    Incorrect. Cycle time is a subset of lead time and refers to the time the team starts working on the task until the task is complete (not until the product increment or bug fix is delivered to the customer). In the scenario provided, cycle time was two days, which is the period of time it took for the team to fix the defect.

- D) Response time

    Incorrect. Response time is the time that an item waits until work starts. According to the scenario, developers spent two days to repair a defect that was found a day earlier. This implies the response time was one day, while the question is asking about the period of four days.

Explanation:

Lead time, cycle time, and response time are terms borrowed from lean manufacturing. Although these terms are typically associated with manufacturing, they are also used by agile teams to measure various metrics on their projects, such as defect repair time. Lead time is the total time it takes to deliver an item, measured from the time it is added to the board to the moment it is completed. Cycle time is defined as the time required to process an item. Response time is the time that an item waits until work starts.

In the scenario described, the team has started to work on the defect one day after it has been found. This one day represents the response time. It took the development team two days to fix the defect. Those two days represent cycle time. It took the deployment team one day to deploy the item (there is no special term for it). The whole four days represent lead time.

References:

Agile Practice Guide – First Edition, Project Management Institute Inc., 2017, Page(s) 61, 64-66

Kanban In Action, Marcus Hammarberg, Joakim Sunden, 2014, Cycle Time

Did you get it right?

Some agile terms are shared among more than one agile discipline, but not these! To get this one right, knowledge of Scrum doesn't help at all. You need to know some Lean Agile and some Kanban, or it's impossible.

And even for someone who studied some Lean, it's still a tough one because:

- None of the four choices is a term that especially sounds like what it means, so all four require being learned and memorized.
- Three of the four terms are related (A, C, D).

The four choices make for a perfect storm in this question! Let's look at why.

Lead time

'Lead time' in waterfall has a very different meaning to how it is used here.

In waterfall, a lead is the opposite of a lag, and the definition of lags or lag time in predictive environments is actually very close to choice D in this question.

In other words, if you build an extra day into the schedule in waterfall, that could be a one-day lag.

But response time is actually the one-day of waiting time in the scenario.

In Lean, lead time has a very different meaning to lead time in a predictive environment.

Actual time

This choice is not related to the other three, but it's not an obviously wrong choice either. It adds confusion to the question because:

- The term 'actual time' (for someone who doesn't know the agile meaning) sounds like it could mean the actual time the bug is being worked on (but that's cycle time – choice C).
- It could also sound like what lead time means, because 'actual time' sounds like it could mean the total time from when the bug was identified to when the fix was created and installed.
- The term 'actual time' is used in agile – as an estimating method, and the opposite of 'idea time'. That's irrelevant for this scenario, but adds confusion since ideal time and actual time in estimating are two ways of measuring the total time of a piece of a project, and lead time is also a way of looking at the total time of a piece of a project.
- 'Actual time' sounds like it could be the counterpart of the waterfall term 'Actual Cost' (AC) used in Earned Value Management (but it isn't). They may conclude that if actual time is the opposite of Actual Cost, that would mean the total time spent to date, which may lead them to select that answer.

The term 'actual time' in English sounds like a better answer than the term 'lead time', but here the question is looking for lead time.

Cycle time

This is close to the right answer, because it's a subset of lead time. However, neither term sounds like what they mean, so it can be hard to remember which one is which even if you study them.

In common English usage, cycle time sounds like it might mean what lead time means, and lead time sounds like time before the work really begins (which is called response time in Lean, or a lag in waterfall).

Response time

Response time is a subset of lead time, so choices A and D are closely related. It can also be incorrectly interpreted as the time between learning of the problem to the time it was completely fixed, but that is not how the term is used in Lean.

Spend some time learning about Lean so you are able to interpret questions like these appropriately on your test. Remember there's an extra bit of abstraction about these terms – they have a mathematical relationship where they go together in a formula:

Lead Time = Cycle Time + Response Time

On one hand, that makes it all the tricker to learn them, but even though you probably won't have to use this calculation on the test, review it until it makes sense and you can recall the formula.

A39 Question 39: Answer

You are managing a project team that has recently been expanded by new team members working remotely from another country. Their roles have been outlined to form a preliminary team charter. Nevertheless, you have noticed a considerable lack of acceptance of cultural differences in the team, resulting in frequent conflicts.

Which of the following techniques could help you in this situation? (Choose three.)

- ☑ **A) Focus groups**
- B) Role definition
- ☑ **C) Ground rules**
- D) Ability tests
- ☑ **E) Meetings**

All answers:

☑ **A) Focus groups**

Correct. Focus groups are an example of individual and team assessment tools and techniques that can be used as part of the Develop Team process implied by the scenario. With this technique, information is collected in group interviews to receive insights on a particular topic. The outputs could help the project manager better understand the root causes of the conflicts in the team and find appropriate solutions.

B) Role definition

Incorrect. According to the scenario, role definition has already been done but did not prevent the lack of acceptance of cultural differences among the team members. The conflict is likely to have deeper underlying causes. A more personal approach is needed to address the situation.

☑ **C) Ground rules**

Correct. Ground rules can be added to the team charter, helping to set clear guidelines for behavior, especially between new team members and within the team overall. Ground rules, as well as codes of conduct, are often proven as an effective tool for reconciling cultural differences in teams.

D) Ability tests

Incorrect. Ability tests are an example of individual and team assessment tools and techniques that can be used as part of the Develop Team process implied by the scenario. These tests, however, are primarily used to assess skills and knowledge of the team members rather than resolve the cultural differences within the team.

✓ E) Meetings
Correct. A team building activity can be an agenda item at a meeting, helping team members work together more effectively. Such a meeting could be used to address the issues and conflicts in the team and to collaboratively find solutions for them.

Explanation:
The scenario surrounds the Develop Team process. This process is aimed to improve competencies, team member interaction, and the overall team environment to enhance project performance. When a team composition changes, conflict is often inevitable, especially when it involves cultural aspects.

A project manager has to demonstrate cultural sensitivity, display strong interpersonal skills, and lead by example. Focus groups, ground rules, meetings (e.g. team building activities) are among the tools and techniques that may help the project manager in reconciling the cultural differences, resolving conflicts, and, eventually, improving the overall collaboration between the team members, thus resulting in better project outcomes.

Reference:
A Guide to the Project Management Body of Knowledge, (*PMBOK® Guide*) – Sixth Edition, Project Management Institute Inc., 2017, Page(s) 340-342, 348

Did you get it right?

This one looks easy from the question, but then there is something tricky about each one of the five choices. Let's look at each of them.

Focus groups
This choice is correct but it might feel too generic for some test takers to select here. Focus groups would be an excellent solution, when you think about what a focus group can do, but they are used in many kinds of situations, notably requirements collection, so they don't sound very specific to the problem.

Equally, they are not a tool of conflict management. As this question centers on conflict management, the test taker may not select it as correct as focus groups are usually used for collecting information. In this scenario, you do need to gather information to figure out the problem and solve it, but if you lean towards focus groups being a vague response, you might not select it.

It's not enough to memorize what a tool is for. You also need to understand what the tools are to the point that you can think outside the box and be ready and able to apply them in cases like this that are not obvious, and not often associated with this kind of problem.

Role definition

Role definition would already have been done, but some Type X managers may read the question and think that more role definition is required, especially if that would be their approach in real life.

Similarly, some managers think that the non-recommended conflict resolution tool of Forcing is their solution to everything. If you are thinking of Forcing here, adding some more role definition is a choice that sounds close. You'll explain everyone's roles to them some more, and that will fix it!

From the PMI point-of-view, role definition would already have been completed, and it would be redundant at best to try to come in and clarify roles now. That would not help at all, and would be ignoring the real issues. It's counter-productive, and lowers morale, to impose the wrong solution.

It doesn't help, it wastes time, and it shows that the manager 'doesn't get it' and isn't a very good manager, hurting their reputation and making the team less likely to listen to their next solution.

Ground rules

Some test takers might think ground rules were already in place from the scenario, which states that a team charter was started.

But that is not correct – the team charter is completed by the team, by definition, and ground rules for and by the team are key to what goes into it. You may miss this response if you don't fully understand what a team charter is and fail to make the connection to ground rules.

To get this right, you need to realize that ground rules, created by the team, could definitely help the problem at the heart of the question.

Ability tests

What do ability tests have to do with solving the problem described in this scenario?

Answer: Nothing!

So why would anyone select it?

Many people unfortunately are xenophobic by nature, and are prejudiced against foreign workers, which this scenario describes.

Even if they are not xenophobic *per se*, they may have a prejudice or even a grudge against outsourcing, often because they themselves might have lost a position as a result of outsourcing or off-shoring work.

Some managers may suggest ability tests to a project manager who finds themselves in this situation, but it would be disastrous, or counter-productive at best, to try to bring in testing to solve this problem.

There's a risk of insulting the foreign workers, as the driver behind the testing is clearly the perception that they lack the ability to do the work. Even if on-shore workers did miss out on the new roles, it's not the outsourced workers fault (it's their own bosses who chose them).

And imagine the results if the outsourced workers scored higher in the tests! That would only make things on the team worse.

Be on the lookout for elements of hidden xenophobia on test questions. It's wrong, and the PMI Code of Ethics and Professional Conduct is very specifically against it.

Meetings
This is another choice that is correct, but might sound too generic for some test takers to select it. You might overlook it if you don't realize that team building activities are considered a kind of meeting or meeting activity by PMI.

That may lead you to conclude that meetings are not relevant to fixing conflict. Meetings that include a team building element would be relevant to this situation.

Question 40: Answer

A40

During iteration planning, an agile coach wants to ensure that her development team has an easy way of organizing their work as well as a visual representation at a glance of the work remaining to be completed in an iteration.

Which of the following tools is best for the agile coach to use to accomplish his goals?

A) A burndown chart
✓ **B) A task board**
C) A burnup chart
D) A glance chart

All answers:

A) A burndown chart

Incorrect. A burndown chart is a visual representation of the project's progress over time. It accomplishes this by displaying the actual amount of work remaining in the project, which will burn down over time. Burndown charts are an agile project team's preferred tool used to display project progress, but they are not a simple way of organizing and managing project work.

☑ **B) A task board**

Correct. A task board is an information radiator that serves the dual purpose of giving your agile project team a convenient mechanism for organizing their work, and a way to see at a glance how much work is left in the iteration.

C) A burnup chart

Incorrect. The burnup chart is the opposite of the burndown chart. The burnup chart is also a visual representation of the project's progress over time. However, it accomplishes this by displaying the actual amount of work completed so far on the project, rather than the amount of work remaining. Burnup charts are normally used to show progress at the project level but can also be used at the release level to reflect any added scope to the release or project over time.

D) A glance chart

Incorrect. A 'glance chart' is not a recognized term used in project management. It's a term made up for this question.

Explanation:

A task board (often called a Kanban board) is an information radiator that serves the dual purpose of giving a development team a convenient mechanism for organizing their work and a way to see at a glance how much work is left to be completed in an iteration. In flow-based agile, the team pulls features from the backlog based on its capacity to start work rather than on an iteration-based schedule.

Iteration-based teams typically use task boards to reflect the work to be completed in an iteration. The team defines its workflow with columns on a task board and manages the work in progress for each column. A task board makes these tasks highly visible so that everyone can see which tasks are currently being worked on versus which tasks are available for selection.

References:

Agile Practice Guide – First Edition, Project Management Institute Inc., 2017, Page(s) 25, 65

Agile Estimating and Planning, Mike Cohn, 2005, Task Board

Did you get it right?

For this question, it's necessary to know that a Kanban board is also called a task board. A lesson learned here is that it's good to know the synonyms also used for popular technical terms.

If you know a little bit about Kanban, this is a pretty easy question. You'll know that a Kanban board definitely answers both criteria that this question is looking for:

- It's good for organizing the work, and;
- It's also a great tool for visual representation of the work remaining to be completed.

Many test takers erroneously believe they only need to know some Scrum for the test, but that isn't the case. You'll also have to know the basics of Kanban and it will also be helpful to learn about other agile methods.

Some people might get this one right through a process of elimination if they know that a burndown chart shows basically the same info as a burnup chart except backwards. The information is not really qualitatively different; it's just a different view.

Therefore, if you see both as choices on a question, like this, you can likely eliminate both, since only one can be right when you are being asked to select a single response. And if one is wrong, the other must also be wrong, unless the question is specifically asking for one of the two.

This tip won't apply to very many questions, but it is worth bearing in mind if you see two synonyms amongst the answers.

Question 41: Answer

A project manager is nearing the end of a product development project for a large consumer goods manufacturer. Several vendors produced key deliverables for the project, and there are no open claims. The project manager is now carrying out all of the activities associated with project closure and is following all project management best practices.

Which of the following tasks should the project manager perform?

A) Close procurements with the vendors
B) Formally sign off the project deliverables
C) Update the enterprise environmental factors
✓ **D) Update the organizational process assets**

All answers:

A) Close procurements with the vendors
Incorrect. Procurements are closed as part of the Control Procurements process, not the Close Project or Phase process which is, as implied by the question, the process being carried out in the scenario.

B) Formally sign off the project deliverables
Incorrect. Deliverables that meet the acceptance criteria are formally signed off and approved by the customer or sponsor as part of the Validate Scope process rather than the Close Project or Phase process. In the Close Project or Phase process, the project manager 'confirms' the delivery and formal acceptance of the deliverables. While the difference is subtle, formal acceptance and the confirmation of the acceptance are two different things. One can think of the confirmation of acceptance as a checkbox that should be ticked during project closure: "Have the deliverables been formally accepted during the Validate Scope process?" If Yes, check the box. If No, there is a problem.

C) Update the enterprise environmental factors
Incorrect. The question implies the Close Project or Phase process is being carried out in the scenario. Updates to the enterprise environmental factors are not among the outputs of this process.

 **D) Update the organizational process assets**
Correct. Organizational process assets (OPAs) updates are among the outputs of the Close Project or Phase process described in the scenario. The updates to the OPAs may include finalized project documents, operational and support documents, project or phase closure documents, and the lessons learned repository.

Explanation:
The question indicates that the Close Project or Phase process is underway. During project closure, the organizational process assets are updated to include finalized project documents, operational and support documents, project or phase closure documents, and the lessons learned repository. Therefore, of the available choices, updating the organizational process assets is the best answer to the question asked.

Reference:
A Guide to the Project Management Body of Knowledge, (*PMBOK® Guide*) – Sixth Edition, Project Management Institute Inc., 2017, Page(s) 127-128

Did you get it right?
This question is very tough, but if you get it wrong, you'll learn what PMI considers project closure.

Here are some reasons why test takers get this one wrong.

- Both choice A and B sound good, and exactly like what someone would expect project closure to be about, so they chose one of those.
- They chose close procurements with the vendors, but this is not part of the Close Project process! Note that when PMI removed the Close Procurements process, it might have been as logical to move this activity to Close Project, but they didn't! This lesson will likely help you on the test.
- They chose to formally sign off the project deliverables. However, it would be redundant to do those things again. The PMI process means they have already verified the scope and the quality, even though signing off the deliverables sounds like a very reasonable activity for project closure.
- Choices C and D look much less correct than either of choices A or B, so they didn't choose one of those.
- They got confused between choices C and D because they look similar, and may have thought that neither could be correct because EEFs and OPAs tend to go together in many cases. They might conclude that if one gets updated here, so should the other.

Being able to answer this question relies on understanding what happens at project closure, and also on understanding the role of OPAs and EEFs.

More on project closure
To understand where the deliverables are accepted, go back to the *PMBOK® Guide.* The PMI Planning processes are largely done in order from top to bottom in the Planning Process Group. Control Quality is done before, or simultaneously with, Control Scope, even though it's down below it in the *PMBOK® Guide* table where the 49 predictive processes are laid out. Validate Scope is done after, or simultaneously.

Next, take a look at Control Procurements, then read Close Project, then go back to Control Procurements again, and you will see this difference between what you expect and what the *PMBOK® Guide* says for this process.

Choice D is very much what project closure is all about, according to the *PMBOK® Guide*, which is still very much the ultimate authority on all points like this, even though the exam is based on content from many reference sources.

More on OPAs and EEFs
One more takeaway from this question is that while it's true that OPAs and EEFs often are inputs to the same processes, something to remember for the test is that it is generally not the case that they both are outputs to the same processes.

Many EEFs are basically only inputs. EEFs could include the weather of the different seasons for construction projects, and government regulations which affect many projects and frequently change.

But they are outside the control of the project manager and project, compared to OPAs which the project manager and team can and should update at the end of projects.

It's a rule of thumb (in other words, not a rule to follow every time, but a useful tip) that OPAs are both inputs at the beginning of processes but also outputs at the end of processes, whereas EEFs are pretty much always inputs. They can and do change, but it's not the project manager or team who changes them.

If you see a question where OPAs and EEFs are in the choices, keep in mind that it's only the OPAs that the project manager might be updating.

Question 42: Answer

During a daily standup meeting, the project manager goes from one team member to another questioning each one on the work they have accomplished and reprimanding them for the slow progress the team has made so far. The meeting lasts for almost an hour and turns into a status meeting.

What should the project manager do differently to avoid the next standup meeting turning into a status meeting?

- A) Use a timer configured to alarm 30 minutes after the start of the meeting
- B) Switch the development life cycle from adaptive to predictive
- ✓ **C) Ask a team member to facilitate the standup instead of the project manager**
- D) Only focus on issues that represent roadblocks and impediments to progress

All answers:

- A) Use a timer configured to alarm 30 minutes after the start of the meeting
  Incorrect. While setting the alarm to a predefined interval may help in adhering to one of the ground rules of the daily standup, this action is unlikely to address the main reason the standup turned into a status meeting.

- B) Switch the development life cycle from adaptive to predictive
  Incorrect. Project managers who have traditionally worked in a predictive environment are used to getting status from the team members. Therefore, switching the development life cycle from adaptive

to predictive will only reinforce the meeting to become status rather than standup. Additionally, the life cycle is typically not switched in the middle of a project.

☑ **C) Ask a team member to facilitate the standup instead of the project manager**
Correct. Agile encourages teams to be self-organizing and self-directing. Having a team member to facilitate the standup instead of the project manager will promote and strengthen this practice.

D) Only focus on issues that represent roadblocks and impediments to progress
Incorrect. Roadblocks and/or impediments to progress are only one of the three topics that should be discussed at any standup meeting. Not only focusing on the impediments is insufficient, but having the project manager leading the meeting and reprimanding the team members for the slow progress is not an agile best practice.

Explanation:
Agile leaders are not only responsible for understanding the guidelines governing the daily standup meeting but also for ensuring that all team members adhere to these guidelines. In this situation, the project manager does not follow these guidelines by allowing the meeting to go over the 15-minute timebox as well as reprimanding the team members for slow progress, thus forcing the daily standup to become a traditional status meeting. Those who have mainly worked in a predictive environment may tend to fall into this antipattern since they used to get a status from the team members.

To ensure that the next daily standup meeting does not fall into this trap, the project manager should empower the team and organize around its strengths. The project manager may want to let the team members facilitate the standup so that the meeting is used as a time for the team to self-organize and make commitments to each other.

Reference:
Agile Practice Guide – First Edition, Project Management Institute Inc., 2017, Page(s) 53-54

Did you get it right?
The more you know about Scrum, and specifically in this case, the morning standup, the easier questions like this will be.

And the more you understand the agile mindset, the easier questions like this will be. That means that PMI-ACP certification holders will likely do better on this question than PMP candidates who do not have the PMI-ACP certification.

Let's look at each answer choice in more detail.

Using a timer
This might help a little. More importantly, there is a rule that standups are supposed to be time-boxed (usually at 15 minutes, maybe 20 minutes according to some agilists). Thirty minutes for a standup is not allowed by the rules of Scrum, so this can't be the right choice.

Switch the development life cycle
Even if this project was predictive, which it isn't, going around the room berating each team member is a very poor way of running a status meeting in a waterfall environment too – besides being a completely unacceptable way to run a standup.

The way to fix a badly-run standup is to do it better, not change the methodology to try to allow the method. That switch would also waste a great deal of time and effort and delay the project, and the reason for switching is a bad one anyway.

Switching to a different methodology to 'fix' a meeting could pretty much never be correct.

Have a team member to facilitate the standup instead of the project manager
This would clearly eliminate the problem of the boss treating the meeting as a status meeting. It would also take away the 'punishment' quality of the meeting, since a team-member would be very unlikely to go around the room berating his fellow team-mates the way the manager has been.

This is a method that is listed as a tip (almost verbatim) from the Agile Practice Guide (page 54) and it's a highly-recommended best practice, for several reasons:

- It's good for team morale.
- It helps each team-member develop facilitation skills and scrum master skills.
- It helps the team remain sustainable.

And there are probably other reasons why this would work that you can think of too.

Only focus on issues that represent roadblocks and impediments
"What are the roadblocks and impediments to progress?" is only one of the three questions each team-member is asked to answer in the morning standups.

Changing the meeting away from a status meeting is a good idea, but it's supposed to be a standup, and as such, the rules of standups should be followed.

The main tip here is to follow the methodologies, in this case the rules of the scrum standup.

Changing a fundamental structure like the scrum morning standup can't be a correct answer on the test, which eliminates choices A and D. Choice A as mentioned breaks the rules of Scrum by using too long a time-box, leaving us with only the correct answer by process of elimination.

Question 43: Answer

A43

To create initial user stories, the product owner is facilitating a story writing workshop with the team and project stakeholders.

What is the main focus of this workshop?

- ☑ **A) To create as many user stories as possible**
- B) To create user stories for the first iteration
- C) To refine user stories in the product backlog
- D) To re-prioritize user stories for the first release

All answers:

- ☑ **A) To create as many user stories as possible**
  Correct. During a story writing workshop, the focus should be on quantity rather than quality, so the meeting participants should write as many user stories within the prescribed timebox of the workshop as possible.

- B) To create user stories for the first iteration
  Incorrect. Although some of the user stories created during the story writing workshop may be used in the first iteration, this is not the main focus of the workshop.

- C) To refine user stories in the product backlog
  Incorrect. The question describes a scenario in which the meeting participants are creating the initial user stories, implying the product backlog does not yet exist. Therefore, there is nothing to refine.

- D) To re-prioritize user stories for the first release
  Incorrect. Prioritization (and re-prioritization) of user stories for a release is done at the release planning meeting, and not at the story writing workshop meeting.

Explanation:

An agile project's initial user stories are often written in a story writing workshop, but user stories can be written at any time throughout the project. During the story writing workshop, everyone brainstorms as many stories as possible. Armed with a starting set of stories, the developers estimate the size of each. During a story writing workshop, the focus should be on quantity rather than quality, so attendees should write as many user stories within the prescribed timebox of the workshop.

References:
A Guide to the Project Management Body of Knowledge, (*PMBOK® Guide*) – Sixth Edition, Project Management Institute Inc., 2017, Page(s) 145

Agile Practice Guide – First Edition, Project Management Institute Inc., 2017, Page(s) 58

User Stories Applied: For Agile Software Development, Mike Cohn, 2004, Story Writing Workshops

Did you get it right?
This is almost a trick question because the right answer sounds counter-intuitive in two big ways, and you might get caught out unless you know scrum ceremonies and scrum principles well.

The two things that might trip you up are:

- 'To create as many stories as possible'
  This sounds wrong, but is right. People are taught to favor quality over quantity in many ways, yet in this ceremony, quantity over quality is the goal. If you didn't know that, you may conclude this is the wrong answer.
- To create the initial stories'
  This would logically suggest choice B to many test takers, because they might conclude that they are creating user stories for the first iteration/sprint.

This is another question where your personal experience may (incorrectly) shape your selection. There are probably many teams around the world who practice some version of modified Scrum or work in a unique hybrid environment who probably do generate initial stories, work on them and then generate some more for the next sprint, and so on.

The question-scenario is really about building the product backlog, although it doesn't mention that term. Choice C is the only choice that mentions the product backlog, which might lead a test taker to conclude that is the correct answer.

The only thing that makes choice C incorrect is the inclusion of the word 'refine' (instead of the word 'create'). Someone who likes choice C because it addresses the product backlog might consciously overlook the word 'refine' and think: "Well, 'create' would be better than 'refine,' and I know there is some ambiguity to watch out for on the PMP test questions, so I'm sticking with C!"

Choice D also sounds pretty good at first glance, because it specifically mentions 'the first release' which the scenario is clearly about.

Again, this choice hinges on one word: 're-prioritize' is wrong. The stories are first being created here, and so they can't be 're-prioritized' if they are only just being created.

However, a test taker might feel confident seeing 'user stories for the first release' and that might make them overlook the wrong word 'reprioritize' or take 'reprioritize' to be loosely the same meaning as 'create', again, given that they have heard there is some ambiguity on the test questions and choices in the exam.

As we've seen in earlier questions in this book, it's important to know a lot about agile and Scrum in particular, to get through the questions successfully.

Question 44: Answer

A scrum master is leading a drug development project for a large pharmaceutical company. She is concerned about the impact of potential changes in the business environment including regulatory, technological, geopolitical, and marketplace, that can impact the product backlog and the project as a whole.

What sequence of steps should the scrum master take to address these changes to the project? (In your exam, on a question like this you would be asked to drag and drop the items from right to left. In this book, please arrange the answer choices in the correct order.)

Answer choices	Answers
Step one	
Step two	
Step three	
Step four	
Step five	

- Assess the impact of the changes on the backlog
- Revise the backlog based on the suggested options
- Identify changes to the external business environment
- Review the environment for any additional changes
- Recommend options for backlog adjustment to changes

Answers:

Answer choices	Answers (correct order)
Step one	**Identify changes to the external business environment**
Step two	**Assess the impact of the changes on the backlog**
Step three	**Recommend options for backlog adjustment to changes**
Step four	**Revise the backlog based on the suggested options**
Step five	**Review the environment for any additional changes**

Explanation:

A project may have exposure to changes in the external business environment that might impact the project scope. This situation is particularly true in highly regulated industries, such as pharmaceutical, as described in the scenario. The steps to addressing these changes, which can be considered risks to the project, follow a logical sequence. First, changes to the external business environment must be proactively sought out as they may not be readily apparent. Once a change has been identified, it should be analyzed and prioritized for the impact on the project and the product backlog.

Although the scrum master is not responsible for the product backlog, she can make recommendations to the product owner. Once the product backlog has been revised to account for the changes, the scrum master should continue to review the external business environment for any additional changes.

Reference:

Project Management Professional (PMP)® Examination Content Outline, Project Management Institute Inc., June 2019, Domain three, Task three

Did you get it right?

This one is a pretty straightforward question, but it's tough because it's hybrid. You have to know the predictive processes of risk management in order from the *PMBOK® Guide*, but at the same time apply the agile concept of the backlog. Both predictive and agile together are being tested, layered on top of each other.

There are also a lot of extraneous detail:

- It's pharma.
- There are of potential changes in the business environment, which can be critical in the pharma industry and can have a big impact on projects and can derail them in mid-stream, including regulatory, technological, geopolitical, and marketplace.

- The question says that the project manager is worried which adds some tension to this question.

The bottom line is the question is simply asking about risk management but hiding it under a situation that sounds dangerous.

This is a good example of how you need to cut out the distractors and just get to the heart of the question, avoiding details that are not needed, and avoiding the emotion or fears of the project manager in the scenario.

In this case the whole question boils down to: "What are the recommended steps for risk management in a hybrid environment?"

There is also some ambiguity about the role of the scrum master, so let's look at that briefly.

More on the Scrum Master role
The question asks: "What sequence of steps should the scrum master take?"

Recommending options for backlog adjustment to changes is clearly the scrum master's purview, but then revising the backlog based on the options is the role of the product owner.

The test taker could well be uncomfortable about identifying the second action (revising the backlog) as part of the scrum master's role, since it really is not, even though the two actions DO logically flow in order as above.

This is ambiguity that the test taker has to push through and not allow themselves to be distracted by.

Sometimes you will encounter some ambiguity on a choice, and you have to let go and choose it anyway!

This is a five-for-five match question, where all five on the left each have to be matched-up with one of the five on the right, and none can be rejected. Step out of the approach you normally take of looking for the best, truest answer and instead step into the approach of matching all the ones on the left to all the ones on the right.

Question 45: Answer

A45

An agile coach wants to ensure that expectations between him and the team members are properly set. The coach meets with the team and emphasizes that he will adhere to the servant leadership approach while working with the team members.

What should the team expect the least from the agile coach?

A) Continuously reminding the team about the purpose of the project
B) Encouraging the team to create an environment where everyone can succeed
C) Focusing on results rather than on a perfect agile development process
☑ **D) Providing feedback on the product increment developed by the team**

All answers:

A) Continuously reminding the team about the purpose of the project
Incorrect. Agile leaders work with the team to define the purpose of the project and the roles of the team members in the project so that they can engage and coalesce around the project goal. The entire team optimizes at the project level, not the person level.

B) Encouraging the team to create an environment where everyone can succeed
Incorrect. Once the purpose of the project is established, agile leaders encourage the team to create an environment where everyone can succeed. An agile coach would ask each team member to contribute across the project work.

C) Focusing on results rather than on a perfect agile development process
Incorrect. While following a 'perfect' agile process is a noble goal, focusing on the product, or the final result of the project is more important. "Working software is the primary measure of progress," states one of the Agile Manifesto principles. This does not mean, however, that the process should be abandoned. Agile teams hold periodic retrospectives to improve the process.

☑ **D) Providing feedback on the product increment developed by the team**
Correct. This answer choice describes an iteration review or demonstration. While an agile coach is one of the key stakeholders to attend the demonstration, it is the product owner, the customer, or the customer representative who is ultimately responsible for providing feedback to the team on the product increment developed during the iteration.

Explanation:
Agile approaches emphasize servant leadership as a way to empower teams. Servant leadership is the practice of leading through service to the team, by focusing on understanding and addressing the needs of team members in order to enable the highest possible team performance. The role of the agile coach as a servant leader is to facilitate the team's discovery and definition of agile. Servant leaders practice and radiate agile. Servant leaders focus on

purpose, people, and process. Providing feedback on the product increment developed by the team, however, is the responsibility of the product owner, not an agile coach.

Since the question is asking about what to expect the 'least' from the agile coach, providing feedback on the product increment developed by the team is the best answer to the question asked.

Reference:
Agile Practice Guide – First Edition, Project Management Institute Inc., 2017, Page(s) 33, 41, 55

Did you get it right?

Here are some reasons why test takers might get this question wrong.

- They might overlook that it's one of those 'what is the least' questions and get caught out.
- They might not understand the agile roles.
- They might get confused by the choice of wording where it doesn't look like the best choice. For example, in this question, the phrase 'continuously reminding' in choice A sounds wrong, but actually it is part of the role of the agile coach. They let the word choice overly dominate their selections and pick the wrong answer.

Let's review some more reasons why this question is so difficult.

Focusing on results rather than on a perfect agile development process

Choice C contains two concepts which makes it especially hard to evaluate. It's difficult enough to 'think backwards' and spot the 'least' answer about one concept, let alone two.

It's also the only choice that includes two concepts, which makes it harder to compare against the other choices.

Sometimes, questions don't make it easy to compare answers, and present choices that are not equal in all respects.

Another thing that makes this a complex response choice is that it is mixing up the core values of the Agile Manifesto.

The Manifesto has four pairs in the format: "We favor X over Y."

But choice C has one concept from the first pair in the Manifesto (Processes) and another concept from the second pair (Results). This will lead many test takers to think about the Manifesto, but that is confusing because this is not a clear copy/paste from the Manifesto.

Finally, if someone is not familiar with the Agile Practice Guide, they might erroneously have the idea that it is part of the agile coach's role to focus on a perfect agile development process.

Key to the agile coach's role is to coach on the agile methods being used on the project, and they may assume that the coach should be trying to ensure the team uses perfect processes. However, this phrase is only one of the two concepts in choice C, which is really about focusing on results and not on a perfect agile development process.

Providing feedback on the product increment developed by the team
This is the correct choice, but let's look at why you might not have chosen it.

It sounds good except for a subtle point about the agile mindset in the phrase: "Providing feedback on the product increment developed by the team."

A project manager who is used to waterfall might read this choice and think that it is clearly the project manager's job to provide feedback on the product, and as agile develops products in increments, they may conclude that it is their role to provide feedback on the product increment.

However, that's not the role of the project manager: it's something the product owner would do.

What looks like the role of the project manager in a waterfall project is not necessarily the role of the agile coach in an agile environment. There's an assumption in some test takers that the predictive team roles map to the agile team roles, but that is not the case. It will be advantageous to study the agile roles really well if you are not confident about them.

A46 Question 46: Answer
As the project progresses and deliverables are being produced, the project manager revisits the stakeholder engagement plan to determine what refinements can be made to the plan to improve stakeholder engagement.

Among the project documents, which will be the most influential to the project management process being performed? (Choose three.)

- ✓ **A) Stakeholder register**
- ✓ **B) Risk register**
- C) Resource management plan
- D) Stakeholder engagement assessment matrix
- ✓ **E) Issue log**

All answers:

✓ A) Stakeholder register

Correct. The stakeholder register is a project document that provides the list of project stakeholders, including additional classification data and other information. This information is essential while planning stakeholder engagement.

✓ B) Risk register

Correct. The risk register contains the identified risks of the project and usually links them to the specific stakeholders as either risk owners or as subject to risk impact. Knowing this information may help the project manager in determining what refinements can be made to the plan to improve stakeholder engagement.

C) Resource management plan

Incorrect. The resource management plan is an important project artifact when developing or updating the stakeholder engagement plan. However, the resource management plan is an element of the project management plan rather than a project document.

D) Stakeholder engagement assessment matrix

Incorrect. The stakeholder engagement assessment matrix is a data representation technique that compares current and desired stakeholder engagement levels. Since the stakeholder engagement assessment matrix is not considered a project document, this answer choice can be eliminated.

✓ E) Issue log

Correct. Managing and resolving issues recorded in the issue log will require additional communications with the affected stakeholders, thus informing the project manager of what modifications should or could be done to the stakeholder engagement plan.

Explanation:

The scenario implies that the project manager is performing an iteration of the Plan Stakeholder Engagement process by revising the stakeholder engagement plan. The stakeholder engagement plan is a component of the project management plan that identifies the strategies and actions required to promote the productive involvement of stakeholders in project decision making and execution. All of the answer choices represent typical inputs to the Plan Stakeholder Engagement process. However, the question is specifically asking for the 'project documents' that will influence the process underway, and the incorrect answer choices are not considered project documents.

Note, the Plan Stakeholder Engagement process is typically carried out during project planning. However, as the project progresses, stakeholders may join or leave the project, warranting an additional iteration of the process. Proactive project managers may want to revise the current engagement strategies even when the project is in its execution stage. In such a case, the Plan Stakeholder Engagement process can be performed again, as is likely the case in the scenario described.

Reference:
A Guide to the Project Management Body of Knowledge, (*PMBOK® Guide*) – Sixth Edition, Project Management Institute Inc., 2017, Page(s) 89, 519

Did you get it right?

This feels a little like a trick question because all five choices are valid functionally, while two of the five are not considered PMI documents *per se*.

Here are some reasons why test takers get this question wrong.

- When they read the last sentence, they focus on which will be the most influential? And conclude choices A, C, and D.
- They miss the word 'documents' which technically invalidates C and D because the *PMBOK® Guide* does not consider them documents. The resource management plan is part of the plan and not strictly a document, yet the resources are considered stakeholders. The stakeholder engagement assessment matrix is key to this activity, yet it's considered a tool and not a document either.
- The word 'register' sounds more like a tool than a document, so they don't select it.
- The risk register and issue log look irrelevant at first glance to stakeholders, but they are relevant and they are documents.
- They didn't read the full question and chose their personal favorite documents or the logical choices, without understanding what the question is looking for, which in this case is three official project documents.

Take some extra time to study categories of terms, like which artifacts are considered planning components versus project documents. The *PMBOK® Guide* provides two tables showing exactly these two sets on page 89. And review which artifacts are considered tools.

In the real world, people think of plans as documents, so it's counter-intuitive that PMI does not.

Question 47: Answer

You are facilitating a risk workshop with your project team to discuss, evaluate, and prioritize previously identified project risks based on the probability and impact of each risk. During the meeting, a key stakeholder proposes that as part of the analysis, the team consider other characteristics of risk beyond just probability and impact.

Which of the following is the least likely characteristic proposed by the stakeholder:

A) Dormancy
B) Propinquity
C) Manageability
✓ **D) Sensitivity**

All answers:

A) Dormancy
Incorrect. Dormancy represents the period of time that may elapse after a risk has occurred before its impact is discovered. Dormancy can be used to prioritize project risks as part of the Perform Qualitative Risks Analysis process implied by the scenario and is, therefore, not the least likely characteristic proposed by the stakeholder.

B) Propinquity
Incorrect. Propinquity can be defined as 'nearness in relationship' and represents the degree to which something matters personally to an individual stakeholder or a group of stakeholders. The more a risk is perceived by a stakeholder as being significant, the greater the perceived propinquity. This characteristic can be used during the Perform Qualitative Risks Analysis process suggested by the scenario.

C) Manageability
Incorrect. Risks can be assessed and prioritized based on their degree of manageability, or the ease with which the risk owner can manage the occurrence or impact of a risk. Since manageability can be used during the Perform Qualitative Risks Analysis process suggested by the scenario, this choice is not the least likely characteristic as asked by the question.

✓ **D) Sensitivity**
Correct. Sensitivity analysis is a technique used as part of quantitative, not qualitative, risk analysis to determine which project risks or other sources of uncertainty have the most potential impact on project outcomes. A sensitivity analysis focuses on evaluating a risk's potential impact on achieving project objectives. However, the goal in the

scenario described is to find characteristics of risk to use beyond probability and impact. Therefore, sensitivity analysis would not be the appropriate technique to use in this situation.

Explanation:

The scenario describes a risk workshop, a technique used in conducting a qualitative risk analysis. However, sensitivity analysis is a technique used as part of quantitative risk analysis to determine which project risks or other sources of uncertainty have the most potential impact on project outcomes. Also, a sensitivity analysis focuses on evaluating a risk's potential impact on achieving project objectives.

Since the project stakeholder in this scenario is looking to use the characteristics of risk beyond probability and impact to conduct the analysis, it is reasonable to assume that sensitivity is the least likely characteristic suggested by the stakeholder.

Reference:

A Guide to the Project Management Body of Knowledge, (*PMBOK® Guide*) – Sixth Edition, Project Management Institute Inc., 2017, Page(s) 423-424, 434

Did you get it right?

This is a tough question because all four choices have merit, and choice D is not obviously the 'least likely'.

As we've seen in other questions, looking for the least likely option is always tougher than finding the most likely response, and it's especially difficult here with the keywords in the answer choices.

There is a further level of challenge because of the somewhat obscure vocabulary being tested here in the choices of the four keywords.

- **Dormancy:** This is a somewhat common English word, but it's not obvious from the word what it has to do with risk. The test taker would have had to learn and memorize it.
- **Propinquity:** This is a very obscure English word. It's hard to spell, hard to pronounce, and very rarely used outside of risk management. If the test taker didn't know what it was, they might guess that this is the correct choice as the least likely.
- **Manageability:** It's an easy word, and it's easy to guess that it means 'ability to manage the risk' even if the test taker is not familiar with it as a risk keyword. Therefore, test takers are unlikely to select this one and it's the easiest to eliminate.
- **Sensitivity:** It's a common English word but the colloquial meaning does not help with the risk management meaning. It's also usually seen with

the term 'analysis'. Sensitivity analysis is a valid thing to do, and so it's only the timing that makes it least likely. If it's going to be done, it would not happen until the next step: Quantitative Risk Analysis (not here in Qualitative).

In addition, it is often a source of confusion for test takers that qualitative risk management sounds very similar to quantitative risk management. Students often have a lot of trouble remembering which is which, and which order they go in by the *PMBOK® Guide*.

And this confusion is exploited in this question.

A way to remember this is to recall that they appear in alphabetical order. Qualitative comes before quantitative, both alphabetically and in risk management.

Question 48: Answer

An agile team uses a Kanban board to manage their workflow. As part of continuous improvement efforts, the team reviews the process they have been using so far to develop the project deliverables. With the help of a software project management tool, the team creates a cumulative flow diagram, as shown below. Today is Day 8 of the project.

Where is the bottleneck in the process?

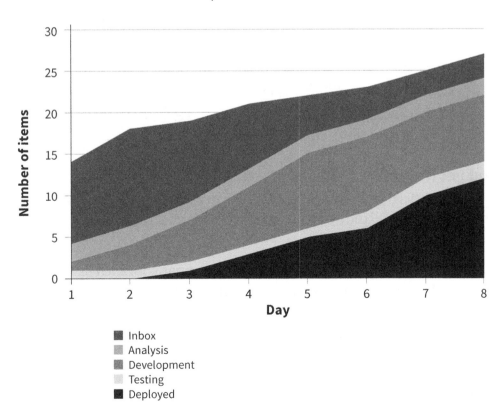

- Inbox
- Analysis
- Development
- Testing
- Deployed

A) Analysis
B) Development
✓ **C) Testing**
D) Deployment

Explanation:

A cumulative flow diagram represents the overall flow of items, such as features or user stories, through the system, for example, through a Kanban (task) board. Each significant step in the process (or on the Kanban board) is represented by an area in the diagram. The cumulative flow diagram shows the number of items at each of the steps in the process at any given point in time.

A bottleneck is what slows or limits the capacity of the process. Wide bands mean that there is a blockage in the flow. Items accumulate as they don't move onto the next step. Narrow bands mean that either work in progress (WIP) of that step is too small or the team is unable to process the items in that step fast enough.

In this diagram, the widest band at this point in time (Day 8) is the Development, which is feeding into a narrow band, Testing. It can be inferred from the diagram and is reasonable to assume that either those responsible for testing have challenges with their tasks, or the WIP of the testing column is too low. Hence, many development items are pending in the Development stage before they can be pulled out by the testers into the Testing stage. Therefore, it can be concluded that in this cumulative flow diagram, on Day 8, testing is the bottleneck in the process.

References:

Agile Practice Guide – First Edition, Project Management Institute Inc., 2017, Page(s) 70

Lean-Agile Software Development: Achieving Enterprise Agility, Alan Shalloway, Guy Beaver, James R. Trott, 2010, Cumulative Flow Diagrams

Did you get it right?

Cumulative flow diagrams are very difficult for many test takers and will probably require more study time for the test than most other diagrams or tools.

Most diagrams in the *PMBOK® Guide* are easy in comparison, such as Pareto charts, where big columns mean big, and small columns mean small: simple!

But unlike Pareto charts, where it's straightforward to compare the columns, the shapes in the CFDs are always all different: one might be skinny at the beginning, fat in the middle, skinny at the end, another might be the other way around, or some other pattern.

To understand the CFD you need to review a lot of parameters and put them together:

- You need to analyze the X and Y columns, like many other diagrams
- You need to analyze each shape, which all have unique sizes and shapes
- Each shape is curved, with an upper and lower line that points to numbers on the Y axis
- You have to look for big differences between the lines of the shapes,
- You have to calculate the difference in numbers between the lines, and at different points on the lines
- You have to look for trending in each shape
- To understand one shape, you also have to look at the shapes immediately below them, as in this question, where that is the key to the bottleneck
- You have to match up which shape goes with which item based on the legend, so that's one more abstraction because your eye has to go back and forth between the diagram and the legend.

CFDs are also very challenging because they are really stacked area graphs. Each individual curve is its own area graph, and it has to be looked at by itself, as well as in its relation to the ones above and below it.

That means the numbers applying to all the curves except the one at the bottom are relative and subtraction of the numbers on the upper and lower lines is needed to get the calculation for each curve.

In the real world, many project managers will have never seen an area diagram before, let alone had reason to read or use a stacked area diagram like the CFD.

There are other things you can be asked about for CFDs besides bottlenecks, and project managers with a strong agile background will find this question easier as CFDs have been part of the PMI-ACP exam for years.

If you aren't familiar with them, find a good resource to use to learn about them for the test.

One more thing that makes this particular CFD tricky is that the analysis curve in this one looks a lot like the testing curve in the same diagram. You may look at the graph and jump right into looking for a bottleneck and get stuck on how these two look similar, missing that the question is specifically asking them about Day 8 on the graph.

It's another case where reading the question is critical.

Question 49: Answer

Defects have been found in some of the project deliverables. The change request to repair the defects has been submitted and approved, and the deliverables repaired.

What should the project manager do next?

- A) Invite the customer to validate scope
- ✓ **B) Conduct the approved change requests review**
- C) Perform the Control Scope process
- D) Request the team to carry out a root cause analysis

All answers:

A) Invite the customer to validate scope
Incorrect. Validate Scope is the process of formalizing acceptance of the completed project deliverables. The verified deliverables obtained from the Control Quality process are reviewed with the customer to ensure they meet customer expectations. However, before the deliverables can be validated with the customer, they usually are checked for correctness first, through the Control Quality process.

✓ **B) Conduct the approved change requests review**
Correct. The approved change requests review is a meeting that should be conducted as part of the Control Quality process to ensure that all approved change requests were implemented as approved. For example, defective deliverables that have been repaired will need to pass through an inspection again to confirm they comply with the quality standards and can be moved as verified deliverables on to the Validate Scope process for the customer's acceptance.

C) Perform the Control Scope process
Incorrect. Control Scope is the process of monitoring the status of the project and product scope and managing changes to the scope baseline. In this case, the change request has been submitted and approved. The work has been done to repair the deliverables. The focus of the project manager should be on quality rather than scope.

D) Request the team to carry out a root cause analysis
Incorrect. While the root cause analysis would likely be required, it is not the next step for the team to take. The scenario presents a straightforward situation where defects have been found and the deliverables repaired. The next logical step would be to verify that the deliverables have been properly fixed. Once it is done, a root cause analysis can be conducted.

Explanation:

The defects that have been found in the deliverables imply the Control Quality process was underway. Change requests can be among the outputs of this process. According to the scenario, the change request to repair the defects has been submitted and approved, and the defects repaired. Once the defects are repaired, the deliverables should be inspected again to ensure they comply with the quality objectives established for the project.

An approved change requests review is an example of a meeting that can be conducted as a tool or technique during the Control Quality process. Therefore, of the choices available, conducting the approved change requests review is the best answer to the question asked.

Note, the defects have been found during the Control Quality process, and the repaired deliverables re-tested as part of the same process.

Reference:

A Guide to the Project Management Body of Knowledge, (*PMBOK® Guide*) – Sixth Edition, Project Management Institute Inc., 2017, Page(s) 305, 164

Did you get it right?

Here are some reasons why test takers get this question wrong.

- They believe choice A looks correct, and logically it could be. A change was made, so why not ask the customer to validate the scope?
- They have not heard of the approved change requests review technique, so they assume it is a made-up term.
- They reason that after making a scope change, some kind of verification would come next, which leads them to select Control Scope as a way to verify changes.
- They are confused because one choice is a process name and one is a technique, and they may not be able to translate the technique to the relevant process.

More on validating scope

In the *PMBOK® Guide*, Control Quality is usually done before Validate Scope. This is a little counterintuitive, as people might naturally assume that first they want to verify the scope, then drill down and do a deep-dive for quality – and there probably are teams that do work that way.

Most of the predictive processes in the *PMBOK® Guide* are done sequentially, but this is one of a handful of times where the processes are performed out of order, according to the chart on page 25. This question exploits one of those 'out of order' exceptions, as Quality Management is several rows below Scope Management in the chart.

Some might ask, "Why analyze the quality results in detail, if you're not sure the deliver was created properly in the first place?"

And that's what the term 'validate scope' sounds like it means: checking the scope. But the *PMBOK® Guide* uses the Validate Scope process to check that the scope was achieved and get the customer's approval on the scope.

To make it even more tricky, the same tool of inspection is used in both processes:

- Validate Scope by inspection, resulting in the Approved Deliverables output
- Control Quality by inspection, resulting in the Verified Deliverables output.

This is one time when a detailed knowledge of the *PMBOK® Guide* is going to help you. Many PMP prep book authors try to streamline the knowledge in the PMI text, because it is so long and overwhelming. PMP book authors also need space in their books for practice questions, charts, graphs, and examples.

However, due to space constraints, they have to leave some concepts and terms out in the process. Some good practices get lost, like the approved change requests review in this question.

A50   Question 50: Answer

The first iteration of an agile project is about to begin. The sponsor gathers the team, the agile coach, the product owner, and other project stakeholders for the kick-off meeting. The sponsor emphasizes the need to identify and respond to the project risks as early in the project as possible and at a minimal cost.

What is the best way for the meeting participants to implement the sponsor's request?

- ☑ **A) The team and stakeholders should frequently review product increments.**
- B) The project stakeholders should conduct risk-based spikes in each sprint.
- C) The product owner and the sponsor should prioritize high-risk user stories.
- D) The team should implement pair programming with the agile coach.

All answers:

✓ A) The team and stakeholders should frequently review product increments.

Correct. In agile projects, the risk is addressed in each sprint as part of backlog prioritization. Once the sprint is over, the stakeholders review the product increment and provide their feedback. This course of action allows the agile teams to increase review frequency with appropriate stakeholders, thus resulting in early risk mitigation at a minimal cost.

B) The project stakeholders should conduct risk-based spikes in each sprint.

Incorrect. Risk-based spikes can be conducted to address project risks. However, these efforts are carried out by the project team members, rather than stakeholders. Additionally, risk-based spikes performed as needed, rather than in each sprint.

C) The product owner and the sponsor should prioritize high-risk user stories.

Incorrect. It is true that the high-risk user stories should be properly prioritized to address risk early in the project. However, this activity is performed by the product owner in collaboration with the team and other relevant stakeholders (including the sponsor, if needed), but not exclusively with the sponsor.

D) The team should implement pair programming with the agile coach.

Incorrect. Pair programming is an agile software development practice in which two team members develop software code in pairs, periodically switching roles and reviewing each other's work in real-time. This practice helps reduce risks as errors are detected quickly. The agile coach, however, is not involved in pair programming.

Explanation:

Agile projects are characterized by frequent changes. Inherently, these high-variability environments incur more uncertainty and risk. To address this, agile practices promote frequent reviews of increment work product and cross-functional project teams to accelerate knowledge sharing and ensure that risk is understood and managed. Risk is considered when selecting the content of each sprint, and risks are also identified, analyzed, and managed during each sprint.

Additionally, projects that experience a high degree of uncertainty and change require active engagement and participation with project stakeholders. Agile projects encourage frequent and continuous engagement with stakeholders, thus helping mitigate risk, build trust, and support adjustment earlier in the project cycle, thus reducing costs and increasing the likelihood of the project success. Therefore, of the choices provided, engaging stakeholders frequently in the review of the product increments developed by the team is the best answer to the question asked.

References:

A Guide to the Project Management Body of Knowledge, (*PMBOK® Guide*) – Sixth Edition, Project Management Institute Inc., 2017, Page(s) 400, 506

Agile Practice Guide – First Edition, Project Management Institute Inc., 2017, Page(s) 55

Did you get it right?

This is a challenging question because of the wording on all the choices.

Let's review the phrasing used to see how it might lead you to inadvertently select the wrong answer.

The question is clear about asking how to reduce risk on this scrum project, but all four choices very much have merit for reducing risk. Choices B, C, and D are all great ways to reduce risk, and they are recommended risk reduction methods, emphasized in the agile books.

However, all three have something wrong about the roles of who is taking the action, so when we inspect them closely, they all jump from responses that look correct to choices that are definitely incorrect:

- The project stakeholders should not conduct risk-based spikes in each sprint.
- The sponsor should not be involved with prioritizing high-risk user stories.
- The agile coach should not be involved with implementing pair programming.

On the surface, choice A sounds like a less direct way to reduce risk than the three incorrect choices.

It is true that the team and stakeholders should frequently review product increments. It suggests (but doesn't state) that carefully reviewing the deliverables after each sprint is important for reducing risks. But at first glance, the other three choices all jump out at the test taker as a more straightforward choice for reducing risk.

Read the full answers, and make sure you understand agile roles really well. Watch out for roles in answer choices because as in this one, the wrong role can override the right action.

PART FOUR

Test-Taking Strategies for PMP Questions

If you have worked through the questions in this book, you will have gained some practical experience of working out tricky problems. This part of the book is going to give you even more strategies and techniques for facing the exam and answering the questions confidently.

In this section, you'll find:

- Tips on how to cope with vagueness of PMP exam questions
- Explanations of the different types of questions you'll meet on the exam
- Tips for answering formula-based questions and for building your confidence with the formulas in the *PMBOK® Guide*
- Tips for working through multiple choice questions and making the most of your time during the exam.

How to Cope with PMP Exam Question Vagueness

Everyone agrees: Questions on the actual PMP exam are vague. Really vague. Here are a few examples taken from actual lessons learned that successful candidates have posted to illustrate the point:

"On the exam day, I was genuinely shocked at the difficulty and seeming vagueness of the questions. [...] I consider myself a fairly skilled test taker (i.e., I'm definitely the good student type); however, I felt uncomfortable with something like 90% of the questions on the exam."

"The questions were mostly situational, and you had to basically pick the best option out of the available ones even though in real life, those may not be the options or decision you would make as a PM. I honestly was not sure of a lot of my answers as the situations were unique and I had to use my best judgement."

"In general, the question info was shorter than the PrepCast and more vague."

"PrepCast had more reference to specific process names, the exam was more vague."

"With my PrepCast practice exam results steadily increasing in acceptable ranges, I was pretty confident in my knowledge base going into the exam. After the first 10 or so questions of the actual exam, my confidence level was at an all time low. Whereas during the PrepCast practice exams I FELT like I was getting 3/4 questions right as I went, during the PMP I had zero feel on if I was doing well."

We see lessons learned like these commenting on the vagueness almost daily, and you may be wondering why we simply add more vagueness to the sample questions in our simulator. The answer is simple: we learned that if we make our questions just as vague as on the real exam, we will be inundated with email complaints from our students. They do not know that the questions on the real exam can be almost irritatingly vague. So, they assume that all truly vague questions in our simulator are 'bad questions' and they will let us know.

Later on, once they have taken their exam, they usually come back to us apologizing and saying, "You were right to include those vague questions!"

We therefore tread a fine line in developing sample questions for the exam simulator that are sufficiently vague but don't cause constant complaints from and arguments with students.

Here are some tips to help you with deal with the question vagueness on the real exam.

1. Be mentally prepared to get lots of vague questions

Nothing can genuinely prepare you for how truly vague the questions on the exam can be. Therefore, going into the exam expecting a large number of vague questions will put you into the right state of mind.

Instead of thinking, "Goodness gracious what ARE these questions?" and going into a panic during the exam, the right mindset will help you stay calm and think, "Yes, this is just as I expected... I can do this!" and power through.

2. Read the scenario and identify the question

This may sound simplistic but reading and fully understanding the scenario and what they are really asking is the first and most important step. If a scenario is vague, then it can be challenging to even understand what the real question is.

One area to focus on and understand is to identify which process or step of the overall project you are currently in. For example, "Are we in initiation or planning?", or, "Is this scenario about quality or risk?" Knowing where and when you are on the project can help you weed out the wrong answers.

Another area to look out for are certain keywords or hints that may point you in the right direction. The best way to practice looking for keywords is to answer as many sample questions as you can and to learn from your mistakes there. You'll get better and better at it.

3. Identify answer differences

Now that you understand the scenario and question, turn your attention to the answers. Often, if you come across a vague question, the answers will also seem vague, unrelated to the scenario, and look very similar to each other, with only the most subtle of differences.

Then again, in some cases even that may be hard, as this student learned: "The four answer options often were all very similar or all felt like they could all be right, and it was up to me to figure out what was MOST right. There were a handful where none of the answers felt right either."

4. Use strikeout and highlight

Don't forget that you have two technical features during the exam to help you:

- The strikeout feature allows you to eliminate answer choices that you find are clearly wrong. ~~The text will appear like this with a strikeout line going through it~~, allowing you to focus on the other answer choices.
- The highlight feature allows you to highlight important keywords in both the question and answer choices. Use it to help narrow things down.

The tutorial at the beginning of the exam will show you how to use them.

5. Trust your instinct

You should be able to narrow the answer down to two choices on most vague questions.

Trust your instinct and pick one.

And in that very moment when you make your choice, take note of how you feel. If your gut tells you that you have chosen the right one, then move on. If not, change your response and listen again to what your instinct tells you. Or, as one of our students said, "I would estimate about 90% of the questions I went with my gut feeling."

6. Mark for review (sparingly!)

If you keep going back and forth between two answer choices and cannot make up your mind, or if you come across a question where all four answers seem correct, then your best option is to select the one that seems best or makes the most sense, mark the question for review and come back to it later.

However, use the mark for review function sparingly. Each question marked takes away time you have available for other questions.

7. If you are running out of time… guess!

Any question left unanswered on the PMP exam will be counted as incorrect. So if you are pressed for time and need to move on, then your best option is to take a guess and pick an answer quickly. At least you have a small chance of getting it right.

Types of PMP Exam Questions

In Part 1, we looked at different types of PMP exam question. That section covered the content of the question, for example, whether it was asking you about a technique. However, there are also different formats for the questions, and you'll see a range of these on the exam.

The different formats are:

- Multiple choice
- Multiple correct
- Drag and drop
- Hotspot
- Limited fill-in-the-blank

Multiple choice questions are like many of the questions you faced in Part 2. You have to select a single correct response from a list.

Multiple correct questions are similar but you have to pick several options, which normally means there are more choices to select from.

Drag and drop questions involve you putting a range of responses in the correct order, by dragging and dropping the choices into the correct boxes on the screen.

Hotspot questions involve a diagram and ask you to select the right section of the diagram based on what the question is asking. These normally involve interpreting data in the diagram to select the appropriate response.

Limited fill-in-the-blank questions require you to type the letter A, B, C or D (whichever is the correct answer) into a text field.

Formula-Based Questions

Recent lessons learned feedback from those who have taken the exam indicates that there are almost no formula questions on the exam. However, PMI updates the balance of questions all the time, so we can't predict exactly what you will see on your test. Having said that, we decided to include a discourse about formula-based questions for completeness.

There is really only one way to prepare yourself for formula-based questions on the exam: study and practice all the formulas. And so you must know around fifty formulas, twenty important values and close to thirty formula-related acronyms. You have to be able to apply the formulas to a project scenario, and if I give you the result of a formula, then you must be able to interpret what that figure means for your project.

But here is the good news... Formula-based questions only have one correct answer. Those PMP exam questions that ask you to select "the best" action or "the next" action often have two or even three answers that seem possible. Not so with the formula questions. Once you know your formulas and understand how to correctly apply them in a given situation, then there is only one correct answer. Because 1 + 1 = 2. Period.

Having said that, there are some things to make your revision and practice easier. There are definitely strategies you can use to improve your recall and knowledge of the formulas. The feedback we receive from exam takers suggests that you might get a couple of formula based-questions, if that. It's unlikely you'll need a calculator and most of the formula questions you face are probably going to be about interpreting a formula result as part of a scenario.

Even so, it's best to be prepared, because PMI changes up the questions frequently. Let's review seven tips for preparing to answer for formula questions.

1. Study the right PMP exam formulas

Over the years, PMI has updated the formulas required for the exam. Make sure the resources you are using reflect the most recent version of the *PMBOK® Guide* so you are studying the correct information.

2. Make a learning plan

It might feel like you'll never get to a point where you know and understand each and every formula, as well as the variations, concepts, terminology, use and value.

But with a learning plan, you can take just one small step every day and practice, practice, practice. You'll soon find that the calculations start to come naturally.

The best way to get confident with the math is to review the formulas regularly. Do sample calculations or questions every other day for two weeks. Take a week off as a break and then repeat for the following fortnight.

As you get closer to your exam date, be sure to answer at least one formula-based question every day.

3. Make a formula sheet

One part of your learning plan should be to make a formula sheet. This is simply a list of all the relevant formulas.

Write down the calculations (try to keep them on a single page). Use this page as part of your regular studies.

4. Make a cheat sheet

The next study resource you can create is a cheat sheet. This is more than simply a list of the formulas. A cheat sheet includes details about what the formula is for and what the outcomes represent. It's a more detailed set of notes about the calculations. You can use it to jog your memory if you can't remember what formula to use in what scenario or how to interpret the results.

5. Make your own flashcards

The third study resource we recommend is creating flashcards. You can buy them, but many students prefer to make their own as the process of making flashcards helps you to remember and recall the information on them.

Use small notecards or cut some cardboard into a convenient size. Write the formula on the front of the card. Write your explanation and notes on the back. Ask your family to hold up a card and you will tell them what the formula is and when it is used – or test yourself!

6. Know how to apply them

Exam success relies on more than simply being able to recall the formulas. You also have to know how to apply them in a given situational question. That could include:

- Inverting the formula
- Applying two formulas: you might have to do this if data you need is missing from the scenario and you have to work it out as an interim step to the 'real' answer
- Interpreting the output of a formula and commenting on the result
- Choosing which formula is most appropriate to use in the scenario: for example, there are multiple ways of calculating Estimate At Completion (EAC) so you have to spot keywords in the question to choose the right approach
- Choosing the relevant data to apply in the formula (and ignoring irrelevant data in the scenario)

Make sure that you know all the earned value management formulas backwards, forwards, inside and out. PMI loves to ask earned value questions!

7. Practice using them at work

The formulas can seem very theoretical unless you have practiced using them in real life. Even if your job doesn't require it, why don't you try to work out the Planned Value, or use TCPI to calculate the cost performance?

Put your new knowledge to use and you'll soon see the benefit of the calculations. This can really help with understanding why you would choose to use one formula over another and can help you select the right data to use as inputs.

Multiple Choice Test Taking Tips

Below, you'll find a collection of multiple choice test taking tips as a quick help guide for preparing for your test. You'll already know that the test includes more than just the simple 'pick one answer from the list' type question, and you'll see questions with charts and graphs, questions where you have to select more than one correct answer, and others where you need to drag and drop answers into the correct order or match them with corresponding phrases.

However, there are likely to be a large number of questions in the multiple choice format you are used to: a range of answers from which you have to select the one best choice.

- Read the question! Look for words like 'least', 'most', 'unlikely', 'best' and so on as these will help you determine what the question is looking for.
- Think about possible answers before you look at the answers provided.
- Read all the answer choices. It can help to read them again in the reverse order to help you take them in.
- Eliminate any answers that you know to be false.
- Eliminate any answers where elements of the answer are false e.g. in a list, one item is false, invalidating the whole response.
- Eliminate choices that mean the same thing: you are looking for one correct answer, so if there are two answers that mean the same, they both have to be wrong.
- Consider eliminating answers that contain words like 'always', 'every', 'none', 'all' 'never' or 'must' because there are very few true absolutes in project management.
- If you have never heard of an answer choice, treat the question carefully – it may be an irrelevant or made-up choice.
- If there are two answers that look similar, you could conclude that one is correct (but don't take that as an absolute rule). Look at the wording carefully to spot what is different.
- Typically, longer answers that contain qualifying words (like 'frequently', 'often', 'sometimes' etc.) are more likely to be right than shorter answers because they are inclusive of more situations or circumstances. However, that's not a definitive rule.
- Remember you are looking for the best answer, not the only correct answer, and not one that must be true all of the time, in all cases and without exception.
- If you truly don't know the answer, guess. There is no penalty for guessing and you will not lose marks. On the plus side, you might guess correctly and gain a mark!
- Trust your judgement. Often your instincts are correct. If you keep changing your answer, you might end up settling on an incorrect choice.

More Tips for During the Exam

Finally, here are some quick tips to help you during the PMP exam.

Answer the questions you are confident about first

Go through the test and answer the questions you are confident about. Mark any question that looks like it will take too long to work out (for example, a complex drag and drop question), and come back to those later.

Substitute words for the correct terminology

Exam questions will sometimes use common or generic terms instead of the "official" name of the formula. Even questions for the earned value management formulas may not use the terminology you are used to seeing. However, use your project management knowledge to infer what the question is asking for. Think about what is being asked, and look for the key data points. Then you can more easily choose which formula to apply.

The format of the answer choices will help you too: if all the answer choices are a financial value, then you know the question is not asking you to calculate SPI or CPI, for example. We have a full article on this topic here: https://www.project-management-prepcast.com/pmp-formulas.

Use the on-screen calculator

When you've practiced the calculations often as part of your studies, you may be able to do the math in your head. However, take a cautious approach and make use of the on-screen calculator that is available in the exam system. Avoid any 'silly' errors by checking your calculations.

Work out your answer first

Read the question carefully and then work out your answer from the data given. Then – and only then – check the answer choices and see if your response is on the list. If it is, great! Choose that answer. If it isn't, go back and make sure you have properly understood what the question is asking. Review what you did and see if you can spot where you went wrong. Then try to work out the answer again and choose the correct response.

> **Tip:** During your PMP sample exams, the mock test should give you the answer as well as the explanation for each correct and incorrect response.
>
> Why use a PMP exam simulator (https://www.pm-exam-simulator.com/pmp-test-simulator)? Knowing why an answer is right is just as important as knowing what you got wrong! This is one of the top benefits of exam simulation software as it really helps students understand the theory behind each response.

If in doubt, guess!

Let's say you come across a really tricky question. You can't see what formula is being asked for and you can't deduce anything from the answer choices. What should you do?

Just guess!

It's a multiple choice question. If you truly have nothing to go on and can't come to a calculated answer, eliminate any response that is obviously wrong and make an educated guess between the selection that remains.

The exam does not penalize you for incorrect answers, so you will not lose anything by guessing – and you might get it right!

ABOUT THE AUTHOR

Cornelius Fichtner
PMP, CSM, PMI-OC Fellow
Founder and President

Cornelius is involved in all aspects of the company. As President and Founder, he defines the strategic direction and works with trainers and coaches to design and develop new products. You probably know him best from his podcasts: he records and narrates lessons for our students.

For Cornelius, no day is like the previous one. He answers student questions in our forums and on email, develops sample exam questions and even edits webpages if needed. During the development of our new products, websites and services he always demands and expects that what we create is beyond reproach. It simply has to be 100% correct but at the same time provide an 'edutainment' factor so that students and customers enjoy learning and using our products.

Cornelius came to project management by accident. He started out as a software developer but quickly realized that he preferred talking to people to writing code. He moved into what was then called "organizational planning" and even became certified in the field. It took him about 3-4 years to make the switch and completely leave software development all the while leading more and more complex and important projects.

Cornelius has been working as a Project Manager in his native Switzerland, in Germany and in the USA since 1990 and received his Project Management Professional (PMP)® credential in April 2004. He has led projects for a management consulting company, a national retailer, an internet startup company, and for one of the oldest financial service providers in the USA.

Cornelius says: "I think the main way I help customers pass their exams is by letting my enthusiasm for project management shine through in our training lessons. Students often comment how I'm able to make a dry subject like PM theory come alive. I'm able to motivate, excite and inspire them on this 'dry' subject, and so they keep going on the road to passing their exam. I'm able to put myself into the shoes of our students and see our products from their perspective. This enables me to create training material that has the customer at heart and will help them to not only prepare for and pass their exams but also helps them become better project managers. I'm the voice and face of pretty much all our training lessons. However, I definitely have a face for radio!"

Cornelius holds PMP and CSM credentials. He currently lives in Tucson, Arizona, USA with his wife and their four computers. He is a member of the American Wine Society Tucson Chapter. He enjoys juggling and says that he is excellent with three balls, OK with four, but can only keep five balls in the air for a couple of seconds.

FURTHER RESOURCES

These additional resources will help you prepare for the exam.

PM✦ExamSimulator™

The PM Exam Simulator
Test yourself and access a realistic, online, computer-based exam environment to answer hundreds of sample questions before heading out for the exam room. Remember to use your exclusive reader discount coupon! You can find out how to claim that from the relevant section at the beginning of this book.

The questions you see in Part 2 and 3 of this book come from here. This simulator is also known as 'PrepCast Simulator' or simply 'PrepCast'.

Find out more: https://www.pm-exam-simulator.com/
Try it for free: https://free.pm-exam-simulator.com/

PM✦PrepCast™

The Project Management PrepCast: PMP Training
The PM PrepCast offers project management training to help you meet your education requirement and pass your PMI exam. Learn with certified instructors who bring their on-the-job experience to help you understand the concepts and prepare for the test. With a range of resources from on-demand learning to instructor-led training, we can help you achieve your certification and take the next step in your career.

Find out more: https://www.project-management-prepcast.com/

Boost Your PMP Score: Learn The Keywords In Sets
Jeff Furman, PMP, PMI-ACP

Available on Amazon: https://www.amazon.com/Boost-Your-PMP-Score-Keywords-ebook/dp/B08SGPGVTK

Oliver F. Lehmann
Project Business Training

PMP Exam Self-Assessment Test
Oliver Lehmann, PMP, ACE

https://www.oliverlehmann.com/pmp-self-test/100-free-questions.htm

Made in the USA
Monee, IL
14 January 2023

25305784R00111